Primary Grade Challenge Math

Edward Zaccaro

Hickory Grove Press

About the Author

Ed lives outside of Dubuque, Iowa, with his wife and three children. He has been involved in education in various forms since graduating from Oberlin College in 1974. Ed has taught students of all ages and abilities, but his focus for the past ten years has been working with mathematically gifted students at the elementary and middle school level. When unable to find sufficient curriculum and materials for his students, he began to develop his own, resulting in the following collection of books.

- *Primary Grade Challenge Math*
- *Challenge Math for the Elementary and Middle School Student*
- *Real World Algebra*
- *The Ten Things All Future Mathematicians and Scientists Must Know (But are Rarely Taught)*

Ed holds a Masters degree in gifted education from the University of Northern Iowa and has presented at state and national conferences in the areas of mentoring and gifted education.

Cover designed by Wilderness Graphics, Dubuque, Iowa.

Phone: 563-583-4767
E-mail: challengemath@aol.com
http://www.challengemath.com

Library of Congress Card Number: 2003106259
ISBN-13: 978-0-9679915-3-5
ISBN-10: 0-9679915-3-6

This book is dedicated to my students, whose passion for math and science is the reason that I teach.

Table of Contents

What's the Next Number?

Mariah had a very difficult choice to make. Mariah was 6 years old and had an allowance of $2 each week. Her mother said that her allowance would grow by $4 each year. This meant that when Mariah was 7 years old, she would have an allowance of $6. When she was 8 years old, she would have an allowance of $10.

Mariah's mother then said something that made Mariah very confused. Her mother said that Mariah could have her allowance increased in a different way if she wanted to. Her allowance could double each year, which meant that when Mariah was 7 years old, she would have an allowance of $4. When she was 8 years old, her allowance would grow to $8.

Mariah now had to choose how she wanted her allowance to grow. Mariah thought that she would have her mom add $4 to her allowance each year because it gave her a better allowance when she was 7 and 8 years old. Just to be sure she was making the right choice, Mariah decided to make a chart so she could figure out which way would be better.

Mariah's age	6	7	8	9	10	11	12	13	14
Add $4 per year	$2	6	10	14	18	22	26	30	34
Double each year	$2	4	8	16	32	64	128	256	512

Mariah was very surprised! She almost made the wrong choice, but when she made the chart she saw that her allowance would grow much faster if it doubled each year.

Predicting is an important part of math!

Look at the different allowances I had when I was younger. Can you guess what my weekly allowance is now that I am 12 years old?

Years	3	4	5	6	7	8	9	10
Money	$1	$3	$5	$7	$9	$11	$13	$15

That's easy! When I look at the pattern, I can see that your allowance increases $2 each year. When you are 12 your allowance will be $19.

Some problems are a little tricky. Look at the problem on the blackboard.

Mel had a jar of 100 jelly beans. He decided that each day he would eat half of the jelly beans that were left in the jar.

Monday.....................100 jelly beans.
Tuesday....................50 jelly beans.
Wednesday.................25 jelly beans.
Thursday...................? jelly beans.

I see how to do that one! I need to take half of 25. Half of 25 is $12\frac{1}{2}$. These problems are fun!

What's the Next Number?
Level 1

1) 24, 26, 28, 30, $\boxed{32}$, $\boxed{34}$, $\boxed{36}$ What are the next 3 numbers?

2) Rachel had these amounts of money in her pocket on the following days:

    Monday...............$10
    Tuesday...............$8
    Wednesday..........$6
    Thursday.............$4
    Friday.................$2

How much will she have on Friday?

3) Gabe is spilling money as he is walking. He started with $100 and then spilled money each mile. How much will he have after 5 miles?

Start: $100
After 1 mile: $90
After 2 miles: $80
After 3 miles: $70
After 4 miles: $60
After 5 miles: $\boxed{50}$

4) 100, 95, 90, 85, 80, 75, 70, 65, 60, 55, $\boxed{50}$ What number goes in the box?

5) 5, 10, 15, 20, $\boxed{25}$ What number goes in the box?

What's the Next Number?
Level 2

1) 4, 8, 12, 16, [20] , [24] , [28]   What numbers go in the boxes?

2) Stacie had $20 on Monday. On Tuesday she had $17 and on Wednesday she had $14. How much money will she have on Friday?

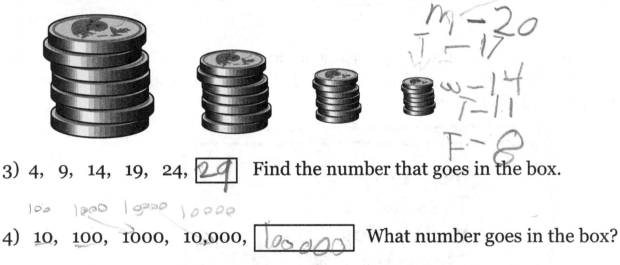

M - 20
T - 17
w - 14
T - 11
F - 8

3) 4, 9, 14, 19, 24, [29]   Find the number that goes in the box.

100   1000   10000   10000

4) 10, 100, 1000, 10,000, [100 000]   What number goes in the box?

5) Carl was saving money for an iguana that cost $26. On December 1st he had $6 saved. If Carl now saves $4 each day, on what day will he have enough money to buy an iguana?

26

December 1st

1   2   3   4   5   6
6 + 4 + 4 + 4 + 4 + 4

6th December

What's the Next Number?
Level 3

1) McKenna had $42 on Monday. On Tuesday she had $36 and on Wednesday she had $30. On what day will McKenna have $6 left?

2) 20, 15, 10, 5, 0, -5, -10 ☐   What number goes in the box?

3) Ben's math teacher played a guessing game with her class every week. She would put a number on the board every day of the week and then have the children guess Friday's number.

Monday   5
Tuesday   10
Wednesday 20
Thursday   40
Friday   ??

4) $1000, $500, $250, ☐   What number is next?

5) How much money did Becca have on Thursday?

Becca's Money

Monday..........$100
Tuesday..........$50
Wednesday.....$25
Thursday.........?

What's the Next Number?
Einstein Level

1) A frog took a magic pill that caused it to grow in a strange way. How much will it weigh at 4:00?

12:00   1:00   2:00   3:00   4:00

1 lb.

      4 lbs.

            9 lbs.

                  16 lbs.

                              ?

2) 9, 3, 1, 1/3, [   ] What is the next number?

3) Meesha's mom bought a pie and set it on the kitchen table. Look at what Meesha wrote each day about how much pie was left. Predict how much will be left on Sunday.

Wednesday....Whole pie
Thursday......1/2 pie left
Friday.........1/4 pie left
Saturday......1/8 pie left
Sunday.........?

4) 2, 1, 1/2, 1/4, 1/8, 1/16, ☐   What is the next number?

5) A magic slug is sitting on a platypus. The snail doubles in weight each hour. If the snail weighs 1 pound at 12:00 noon, at what time will the snail weigh 128 pounds?

Don't Let it Break

Ted was looking forward to the party on the last day of school. He was especially looking forward to the rope-pulling contest between his school and Einstein Elementary School.

During the rope-pulling contest, 200 students from each school would stand on separate sides of a rope that was 1000 feet long. Each team would then try to pull the other team across the finish line.

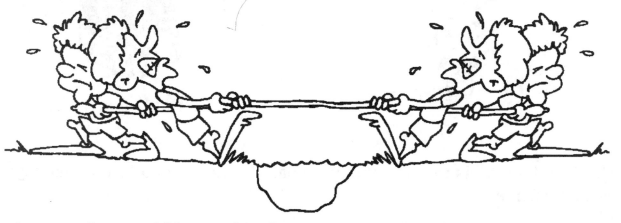

The rope that would be used in the contest was placed out in the playground so all the children could look at it and then read some information about the rope. Ted was excited as he ran out to look at the rope and read the information.

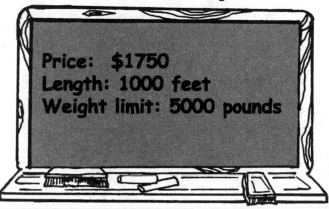

Price: $1750
Length: 1000 feet
Weight limit: 5000 pounds

After Ted read about the rope, he became very upset. Ted was always doing math problems in his head and he had just figured out that if 200 children from his school each pulled with a force of 50 pounds, they would be putting 10,000 pounds of force on the rope. By using math, Ted found out that the rope was in danger of breaking during the rope-pulling contest!!

After Ted explained his math to the principal, it was decided to only have 50 children on each team.

Because Ted used math to stop an accident, he was presented with an Einstein Award to honor his brilliant thinking.

Don't Let it Break
Level 1

1) Jake's bike has a weight limit of 200 pounds. If he weighs 150 pounds, can he bring his 55 pound dog on the bike with him?

2) Giant ants are carrying eggs across a thin branch. Each ant weighs 1 pound and each egg weighs 4 pounds. If the branch can safely hold only 25 pounds, how many egg-carrying ants can cross the branch together?

3) A rope swing will safely hold 500 pounds. How many 50 pound children can safely sit on the rope swing?

4) A 400 pound gorilla is going to carry a 585 pound rock across a bridge that can safely hold 1000 pounds. Is this a safe amount of weight?

5) Emily built a toothpick bridge that was strong enough to hold 15 pounds. How many $2\frac{1}{2}$ pound rats can sit on the bridge without it breaking?

Don't Let it Break
Level 2

1) It is dangerous to put too much weight in a canoe. If the safety limit of a canoe is 600 pounds, how many 175 pound people can you place in it?

2) A sign on a truck said that you must not put more than one ton into the truck. If a can of peaches weighs 2 pounds, how many cans of peaches can you put into the truck?

Did you know that 1 ton = 2000 pounds?

3) The floor at a paint store will collapse if too many big cans of paint are put in one spot. If each big can of paint weighs 100 pounds, how many cans of paint can you safely place by the sign?

No more than 1000 pounds to be put here

4) Chicken Little had an acorn fall on her head and she went down the road telling everyone the sky was falling. While she did that, her sister collected acorns and put them in her backpack. If each acorn weighs 2 ounces, and the backpack will only hold 2 pounds, how many acorns can Chicken Little's sister put in her backpack?

Did you know that there are 16 ounces in a pound?

5) If a rope hanging from a gym ceiling can safely hold 1000 pounds, how many 50 pound children can be on the rope at the same time?

Don't Let it Break
Level 3

1) Ben has a paper route. When he carries the Sunday paper his backpack is very heavy and Ben ends up with very sore shoulders. Ben decided that he would not put more that 20 pounds in his backpack. If each paper weighs 1/3 of a pound, how many papers can he carry in his backpack?

2) All 500 children from Einstein Elementary School were standing on a bridge for a group picture. While Rachel was waiting for the picture to be taken, she noticed a sign on the bridge.

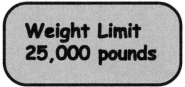

Weight Limit
25,000 pounds

Rachel knew that the average weight of a student at the school was 60 pounds. Should Rachel be worried about too much weight on the bridge?

3) The deck at McKenna's house is safe as long as it has no more than 2000 pounds on it. If each person weighs 125 pounds, how many people can safely be on the deck?

4) A 1/2 ton elephant is standing on a scale. The elephant is holding a 1 pound rat and the rat is holding a 1 ounce worm. The scale is a strange scale that only weighs in ounces. How many ounces does the scale say?

Remember, there are 16 ounces in a pound

5) A chair can only hold 100 pounds. If Dave weighs 2000 ounces, can he safely sit in the chair?

Don't Let it Break
Einstein Level

1) A bridge has a sign by it that says it can safely hold 5 cars that each weigh 3000 pounds. If no cars are on the bridge, how many 150 pound people can safely stand on the bridge?

2) Rapunzel is a fairy tale about a girl with long hair who was trapped in a tower. A witch would make Rapunzel hang her hair out the window so she could climb up the tower.

Remember, there are 16 ounces in a pound.

Each strand of Rapunzel's hair could hold 4 ounces. If Rapunzel had 1000 strands of hair, could a 200 pound witch safely climb up Rapunzel's hair?

3) A quarter is 1/15 of an inch thick and 5 quarters weigh one ounce. Stephanie built a toothpick bridge that could safely hold 3 pounds. Stephanie wanted to make a tall tower of quarters on her bridge. What is the highest her quarter tower could be and not go over 3 pounds?

4) If more than 720 pounds of water are put into a bathtub at Anna's house, the floor is in danger of breaking. How many pints of water can Anna safely put into her bathtub?

5) A bridge has a warning sign that says: "No trucks over 20,000 pounds are allowed to cross." Look at the list below and then decide how many bags of sand can be safely taken across the bridge.

How Much Does it Cost?

Amy needed to buy candy bars for a party, so she visited her local grocery store. When she arrived at the aisle where the candy bars were kept, she saw a sign with the price of the candy bars on it.

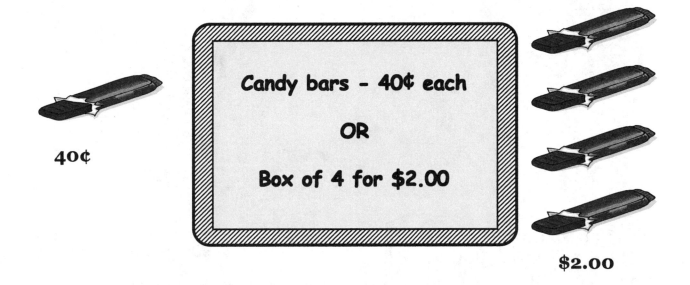

40¢

Candy bars - 40¢ each

OR

Box of 4 for $2.00

$2.00

Amy needed 20 candy bars, so she picked up 5 boxes that each had four candy bars. As Amy walked toward the cashier, something started bothering her. Amy knew that most of the time if you buy more of something you get a better price. That was why she bought the candy bars in packages of 4.

Amy did some math in her head and then decided to buy the single candy bars that were 40¢ each.

How Much Does it Cost?
Level 1

1) Which is a better deal, 4 pet alligators for $20.00 or 5 for $24.00?

2) It cost $4.50 to visit a killer whale. What would it cost for 4 people to visit a killer whale?

3) If a pound of bananas cost 40¢ , what does 1/4 pound of bananas cost?

Did you know that there are 16 ounces in a pound?

4) Chocolate covered peanuts cost 50¢ per ounce. How much would a pound cost?

5) Honey cost $4.25 per jar. If Erin bought 4 jars, how much change would she get from a $20 bill?

How Much Does it Cost?
Level 2

1) If a dozen donuts cost $3.00, how much does each donut cost?

Did you know that a dozen means 12?

2) If a pound and a half of raisins cost $1.50, how much does a pound of raisins cost?

3) If a 15 inch stack of tuna cans cost $3.50, how much does a 45 inch stack cost?

4) Which is a better buy, 5 candy bars for 80¢ or 4 candy bars for 60¢?

5) Rich bought six 30¢ stamps. How much change did he get from a $20 bill?

How Much Does it Cost?
Level 3

1) A pet store was having a going out of business sale. The price of a snake was $100 on Monday, $50 on Tuesday, and $25 on Wednesday. Each day the store kept cutting the price in half. If Steve had $3.50, on what day will he have enough money to buy the snake?

2) A pencil and a pen together cost $1.20. If the pen cost twice as much as the pencil, how much does the pencil cost?

3) If 3 ounces of peanuts cost 60¢, what would a pound of peanuts cost?

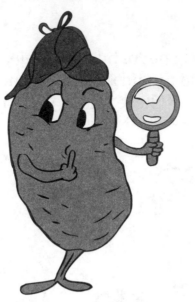

4) Bumper cars cost $12 for a half hour. How much does 20 minutes cost?

5) Store A sells ice cream cones for $1.50 each. Store B sells ice cream cones for $1.75 each, but they give you a free cone after you buy 5. If you want 6 ice cream cones, which store has a better deal?

How Much Does it Cost?
Einstein Level

1) A hot dog and candy bar together cost $5.00. If the price of the hot dog is $4 more than the candy bar, what is the price of the candy bar?

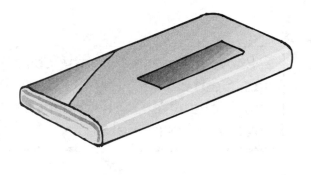

2) Derek's family is going on vacation. The family car can go 20 miles with one gallon of gas. If gas cost $1.50 for each gallon, how much will gas cost for a 1000 mile trip?

3) If the price of a gallon of milk is $2.56, how much does a cup of milk cost?

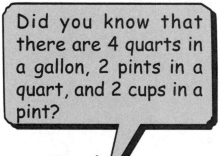

Did you know that there are 4 quarts in a gallon, 2 pints in a quart, and 2 cups in a pint?

4) The cost of electricity to run a heater in Luke's room is 15¢ per hour. How much will it cost if Luke's heater is on for the month of December?

5) If a meter of golden chain cost $1000, how much does a centimeter of golden chain cost?

How Much Change Will I Get?

Selena went to the pet store with her mother and father to buy a dog. The dog she picked out was very cheap because it had been in the store for a long time.

It's about time somebody picked me. I'm getting tired of living in a cage!

When they went to pay for the dog, the store clerk told them that the total cost was $15.12. Selena's mom gave the clerk a $20 bill and also a dime and two pennies.

Selena was very confused. "Why did you give the clerk $20.12 if the dog only cost $15.12?" Before her mom could answer, the clerk gave Selena's mom $5 in change. "Now I know why you gave the clerk $20.12. It was easier to make change that way!"

Sometimes you can figure out how much change you'll get without using paper or a calculator.

If I bought a hat for $17.20 and gave the clerk a $20 bill, how much change would I get?

First think how much money in coins you would get. Here it is pretty easy to see that you would get 80¢.

That makes it simple. Now it is easy to see that I will also get $2.

That was very clever of you Einstein. Now it is easy to see that the change will be 75¢ plus one dollar. The answer is $1.75!

Stan bought a baseball for $3.27. He gave the clerk $5.02. How much change will he get?

Try to solve the following problems in your head.

How Much Change Will I Get?
Level 1

1) Noah bought a safe that cost $80.25.
He gave the clerk at the store $100.25.
How much change will he get?

2) Stephanie bought an item that cost $17.03. She gave the clerk a $20 bill and some coins. What coins did Stephanie give to the clerk to make it easier to make change?

3) Warren bought a fiddle playing ant for $99.10. How much change did he get from a $100 bill?

4) Mike bought a candy bar for 78¢. When he gave the clerk a $1 bill, she gave him a quarter in change. Mike knew this was too much change so he left some money on the counter. How much money did Mike leave?

5) Alex bought a soccer ball for $17.50. He gave the clerk a $20 bill and asked for his change in dimes. How many dimes should Alex get?

How Much Change Will I Get?
Level 2

1) If Stephanie buys a pet mouse for $12.50 and gives the clerk a $20 bill, how much change will she get?

2) Belinda bought a bag of dog food for $5.10. She gave the clerk $6.25. How much change will she get?

3) The price of a book is $7.12. In your pocket is a $10 bill and a lot of coins. What amount of money would you give to the clerk to make it easier to make change?

4) Shirley bought a pencil and eraser that cost $1.77. She paid for it with a $2 bill plus 2 pennies. What would be Shirley's change?

5) The price of a stuffed Panda Bear is $13.40. If you paid with a $20 bill, how much change would you receive?

How Much Change Will I Get?
Level 3

1) Dave bought a rag doll for $8.47. He gave the clerk $10.02. How much change will he get?

2) Nancy bought a stuffed turtle for $11.12 and gave the clerk $21.15. How much change will she get?

3) Steve bought a guitar for $93.87. He gave the clerk a $50 bill, two $20 bills, and a $5 bill. Steve then gave the clerk 2 pennies. Why did Steve give the clerk 2 pennies?

4) A CD normally cost $17.95, but today it is $5 off. If Rachel bought a CD and paid for it with a $100 bill, how much change will she get?

5) Kenny paid $91.47 for used maracas. He gave the clerk a $100 bill plus 47¢. How much change will he get?

How Much Change Will I Get?
Einstein Level

1) Soccer balls are $9.99 each. If Ruth bought 10 soccer balls and gave the clerk a $100 bill, how much change will she get?

2) Amy bought a $90 harp with her coin collection. In her collection she had one hundred 1/2 dollars, 100 quarters, 100 dimes, 100 nickels, and 100 pennies. How much change will Amy get?

3) In the year 2002, a Canadian dollar was not worth as much as a dollar from the United States. If a Canadian dollar is worth 75¢ of United States money and you are in Canada buying a $10 movie ticket, how much will you pay in United States money?

4) A rat cost 99¢, a turtle cost $9.99, a dog cost $99.99, and a parrot cost $999.99. If you paid for the animals with 12 $100 bills, how much change would you get?

5) Garth always tried to confuse story clerks when he bought things. Yesterday Garth bought a $12.82 statue called the pointing Monkey. He gave the clerk $25.32. How much change should Garth receive?

Balance it

Clara was excited about the new seesaw that just arrived at her school's playground. This seesaw was special because it had comfortable seats on each end where she and her friend May could sit.

Clara was looking forward to using the seesaw the next day, but she was worried. Clara weighed 72 pounds and May weighed 69 and 1/2 pounds. When Clara would seesaw with May, she always moved up her side of the seesaw because she weighed more. But she didn't want to do that on the new seesaw because that would mean she couldn't sit on the comfortable seat.

Clara thought of an idea. What if she could make May the same weight as her? If she could, then they would be perfectly balanced and they both could sit on the comfortable seats. Clara started thinking of ways to make May weigh the same as her. The first thing she thought of was to buy a lot of fudge and candy bars to make May gain some weight, but Clara knew that was a silly idea.

Clara thought about the problem all day before she realized what she could do. She would have May put enough sand in her pockets to make both of them weigh the same.

The next day May came over to Clara's house. Clara got out her scale and weighed out 1 pound of sand and put it into May's pocket. Now May weighed 70 1/2 pounds. Clara then weighed out another 1 pound of sand. Now May weighed 71 1/2 pounds.

Clara was a little confused because if she put another pound of sand in May's pocket, she would weigh too much. After a little thinking, Clara realized that if she put a half pound of sand in May's pocket, her weight would be exactly 72 pounds.

Balance it
Level 1

1) How much weight would you add to the right side to balance the board?

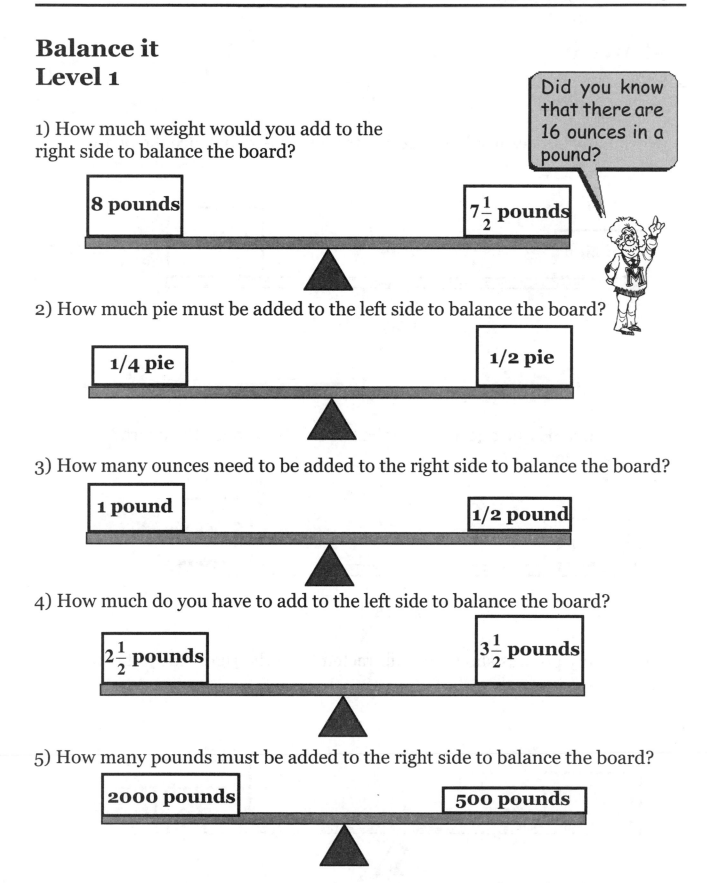

2) How much pie must be added to the left side to balance the board?

3) How many ounces need to be added to the right side to balance the board?

4) How much do you have to add to the left side to balance the board?

5) How many pounds must be added to the right side to balance the board?

Balance it
Level 2

1) How many ounces would you add to the left side to balance the board?

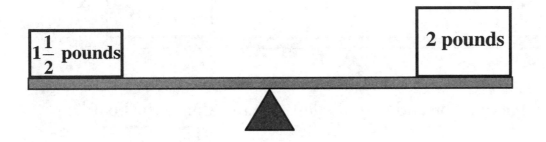

2) How much pie must be added to the left side to balance the board?

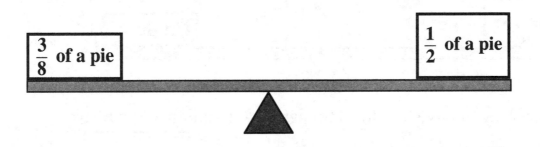

3) How many pounds should be subtracted from the right side to balance the board?

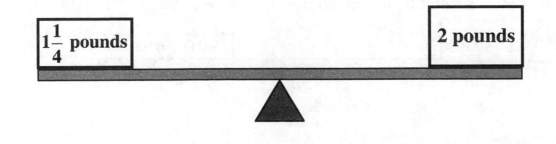

4) How much do you have to add to the left side to balance the board?

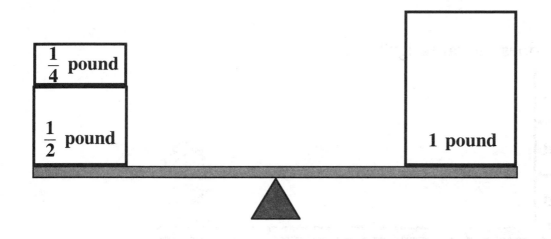

5) How many pounds must be added to the right side to balance the board?

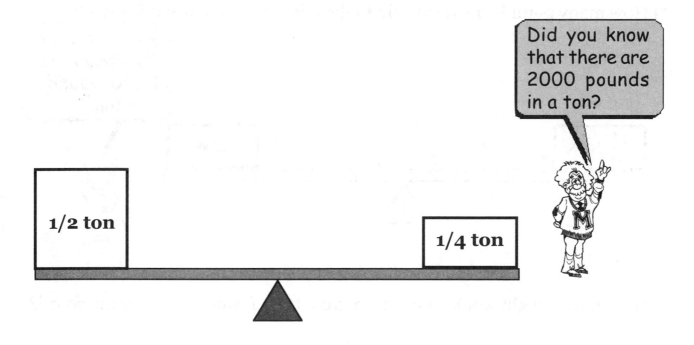

Balance it
Level 3

1) How much does the rat weigh?

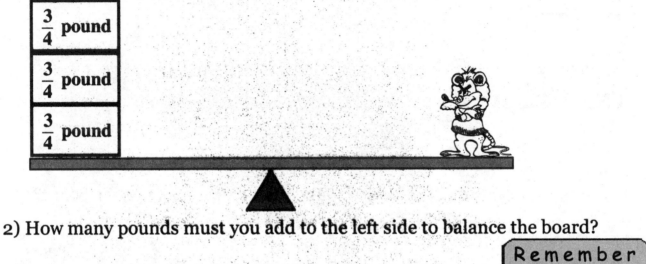

2) How many pounds must you add to the left side to balance the board?

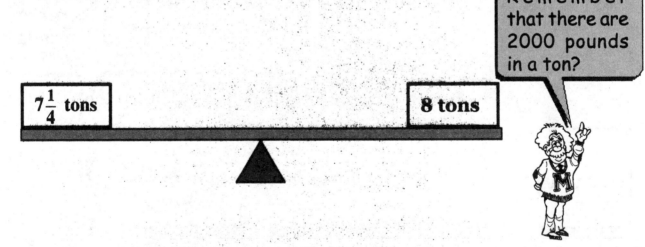

Remember that there are 2000 pounds in a ton?

3) How much weight would you remove from the left side to balance the board?

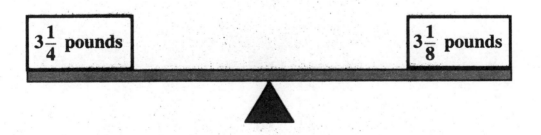

4) What part of a pie must be added to the left side to balance the board?

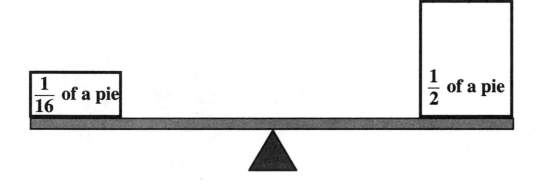

5) A 70 pound child wants to balance on a seesaw with a 140 pound adult. If the child sits at the end of the board, where should the adult sit to balance the board?

Balance it
Einstein Level

1) How many ounces does Luke's rat weigh?

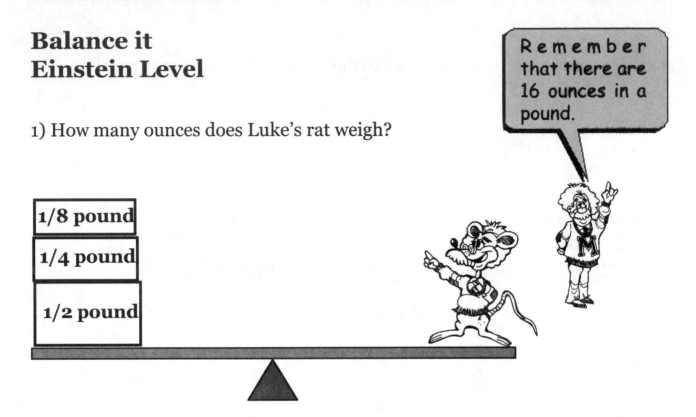

2) How much weight would you add to the left side to make the board balance?

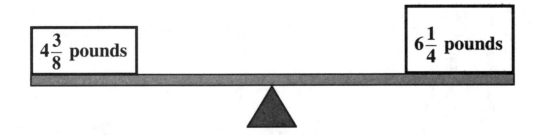

3) How many ounces need to be added to the left side to balance the board?

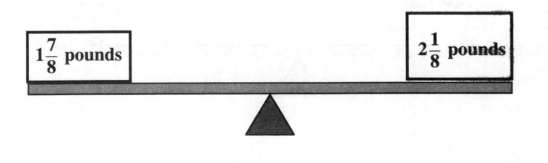

4) **How many pounds must you add to the left side to balance the scale?**

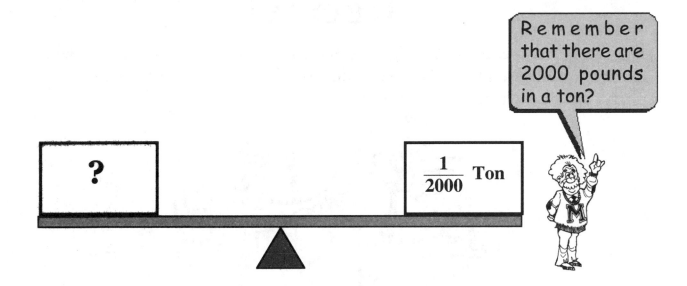

5) **How many pints do you need to place on the left side to balance the scale?**

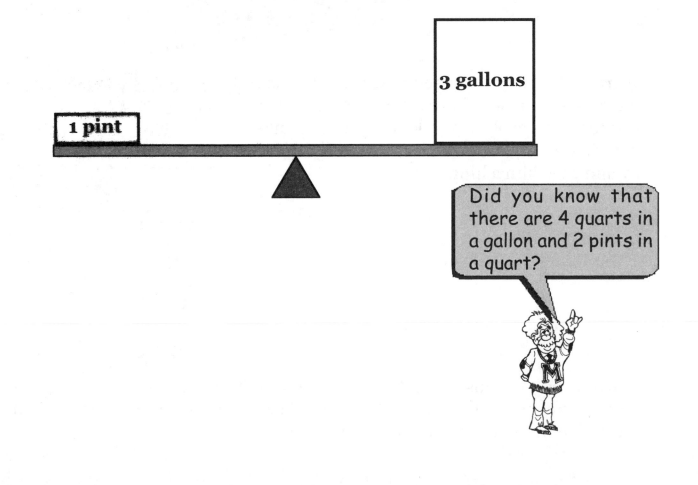

Oh No, I have to Change the Recipe!

Warren loved to cook, but tonight he had a problem. After he finished cooking a chicken, he needed to make 30 cookies to bring to school for his class birthday party, but his favorite recipe only made 20 cookies.

Warren thought to himself that if he doubled the recipe he would have 40 cookies, but that was too many cookies. While Warren was thinking of a way to get 30 cookies, Einstein stopped by and gave him a hint.

How could you make 10 cookies? What would you have to do to the recipe?

Warren knew the answer to that. To make 10 cookies, he would cut the recipe in half. Warren wrote the recipe on the blackboard and then he wrote what half of the recipe would be on another blackboard.

Recipe for 20 Cookies

$2\frac{1}{2}$ cups of oatmeal

1 cup of flour

$\frac{1}{2}$ cup of oil

1 cup of brown sugar

$1\frac{1}{2}$ cups of raisins

1 teaspoon of baking powder

$\frac{1}{2}$ cup of water

I'll now cut this recipe in half so I can make 10 cookies.

That's a great idea. Then you will have two recipes. One for 20 cookies and one for 10 cookies.

Recipe for 10 Cookies

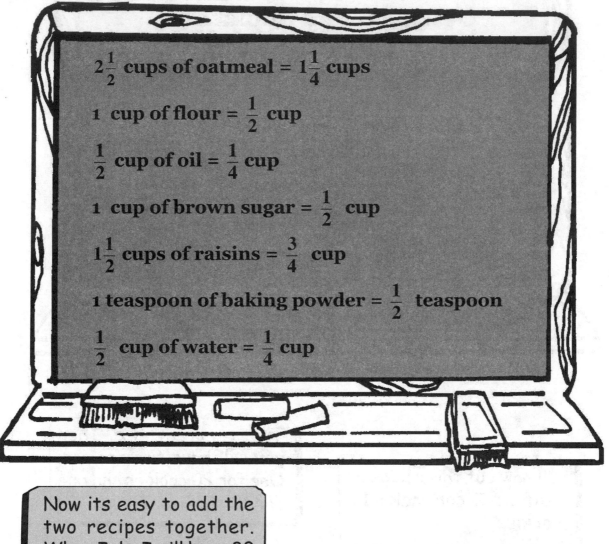

$2\frac{1}{2}$ cups of oatmeal = $1\frac{1}{4}$ cups

1 cup of flour = $\frac{1}{2}$ cup

$\frac{1}{2}$ cup of oil = $\frac{1}{4}$ cup

1 cup of brown sugar = $\frac{1}{2}$ cup

$1\frac{1}{2}$ cups of raisins = $\frac{3}{4}$ cup

1 teaspoon of baking powder = $\frac{1}{2}$ teaspoon

$\frac{1}{2}$ cup of water = $\frac{1}{4}$ cup

Now its easy to add the two recipes together. When I do, I will have 30 cookies!

Recipe for 30 Cookies

$2\frac{1}{2}$ cups of oatmeal $+ 1\frac{1}{4}$ cups $= 3\frac{3}{4}$ cups

1 cup of flour $+ \frac{1}{2}$ cup $= 1\frac{1}{2}$ cups

$\frac{1}{2}$ cup of oil $+ \frac{1}{4}$ cup $= \frac{3}{4}$ cup

1 cup of brown sugar $+ \frac{1}{2}$ cup $= 1\frac{1}{2}$ cups

$1\frac{1}{2}$ cups of raisins $+ \frac{3}{4}$ cup $= 2\frac{1}{4}$ cups

1 teaspoon of baking powder $+ \frac{1}{2}$ teaspoon $= 1\frac{1}{2}$

$\frac{1}{2}$ cup of water $+ \frac{1}{4}$ cup $= \frac{3}{4}$ cups

Wait until the class hears how I changed the recipe to make 30 cookies.

You're so smart that it scares me sometimes.

Oh No, I have to Change the Recipe!
Level 1

1) If 50 cookies need 5 eggs, how many eggs would you need to make 150 cookies?

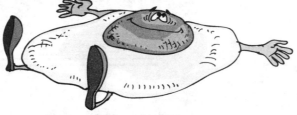

2) If you want to triple a recipe that calls for 9 apples, how many apples would you need?

3) If a 15 pound chicken will feed 30 people, how many people will a 5 pound chicken feed?

4) If a recipe that makes 90 cookies calls for 6 cups of oats, how many cups of oats would you use for 30 cookies?

5) A 10 pound cake uses 3 cups of sugar. How many cups of sugar would a 5 pound cake use?

Oh No, I have to Change the Recipe!
Level 2

1) If 40 cookies need $2\frac{1}{2}$ cups of flour, how much flour would you need to make 20 cookies?

2) If you want to double a recipe that calls for $2\frac{1}{2}$ apples, how many apples would you need?

3) A box of Cheerios will last 6 days for 2 people. How long will the box last for 6 people?

4) A recipe for 20 chocolate bars calls for 1/2 teaspoon of salt. If you are going to make 10 chocolate bars, how much salt would you use?

5) Pedro needed 75 cookies, but his favorite recipe for oatmeal cookies only made 25 cookies. Look at the recipe for 25 cookies and write down the new amounts for 75 cookies.

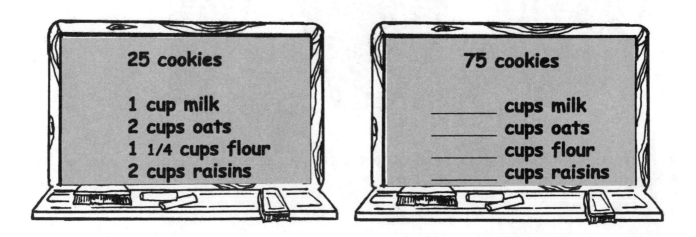

25 cookies

1 cup milk
2 cups oats
1 1/4 cups flour
2 cups raisins

75 cookies

_____ cups milk
_____ cups oats
_____ cups flour
_____ cups raisins

Oh No, I have to Change the Recipe!
Level 3

1) If 10 cookies use $1\frac{1}{3}$ cups of raisins, how many cups of raisins would you use for 30 cookies?

2) If a 10 pound cake needs 4 eggs, how many eggs would you need for a 25 pound cake?

3) If 1 pound of spaghetti will feed 4 people, how many people will $2\frac{1}{2}$ pounds feed?

4) A loaf of French bread will last $2\frac{1}{2}$ days for 3 people. How long will the loaf last for 1 person?

5) A recipe for a 2 pound cake calls for 1/4 teaspoon of baking powder. If you make a 1 pound cake, how much baking powder should you use?

Oh No, I have to Change the Recipe!
Einstein Level

1) A recipe for 50 banana cookies uses $1\frac{1}{2}$ pounds of bananas. How many pounds of bananas would you need if you wanted to make 75 banana cookies?

2) A box of Shredded Wheat will last 12 days for 3 people. How long will it last for 4 people?

2) If 20 people need 10 gallons of milk per week, how many people would $2\frac{1}{2}$ gallons of milk serve for a week?

4) Ben found a recipe for 40 pancakes that called for 10 eggs. If Ben only wants to make 5 pancakes, how many eggs should he use?

5) While Eric was making a cake, he put 5 cups of flour into the mixing bowl instead of the 4 cups the recipe called for. Now he has to change all the other amounts in the recipe. What are the new amounts?

Recipe	
Flour	4 cups
Sugar	1 cup
Oats	2 cups

Changed Recipe	
Flour	5 cups
Sugar	? cups
Oats	? cups

The Magic of Multiplying

Kyle had a problem. He had a summer job working at a place that made candy bars. Part of his job was to let his boss know how many candy bars were loaded on trucks every hour. This is where Kyle's problem started. Each bag of candy bars contained 95 candy bars. Kyle watched bag after bag as they were loaded onto a truck. As he watched, Kyle counted the bags and then made an addition problem.

Because there were 40 bags of candy bars loaded on the truck, Kyle's addition problem was so large that it began to give him a headache. He knew there had to be a better way to count the candy bars.

$$
\begin{array}{r}
95 \\
95 \\
95 \\
95 \\
95 \\
95 \\
95 \\
95 \\
95 \\
95 \\
+\ 95 \\
\hline
\end{array}
$$

Another way to do multiplication is by using a calculator.

If you had 81 bags of money with $42 in each bag, you wouldn't want to add $42, 81 times. All you need to do is multiply 81 x 42 = $3,402.

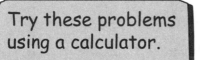

Try these problems using a calculator.

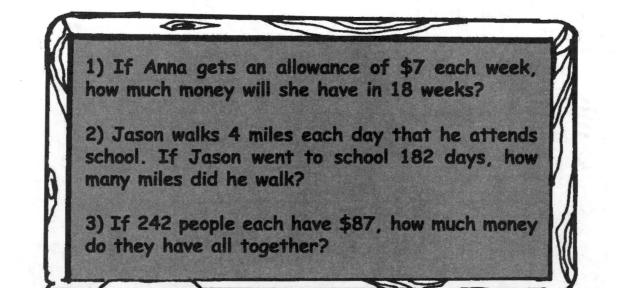

1) If Anna gets an allowance of $7 each week, how much money will she have in 18 weeks?

2) Jason walks 4 miles each day that he attends school. If Jason went to school 182 days, how many miles did he walk?

3) If 242 people each have $87, how much money do they have all together?

Another way to multiply is by using pencil and paper. This takes a little practice to learn. Look at how I do 842 x 6.

Step 1:	842 x 6
Step 2:	1 842 x 6 ――― 2
Step 3:	2 1 842 x 6 ――― 5 2
Step 4:	2 1 842 x 6 ――― 5052

6 x 2 is 12 so you put the 2 down and carry the 1.

6 x 4 is 24 plus the 1 you carried is 25. You put the 5 down and carry the 2.

6 x 8 is 48 plus the 2 you carried is 50.

842 x 6 = 5052

Try these problems using paper and pencil.

If 9 cats each had 22 fleas, how many fleas would there be all together?

482 children each read 5 books. How many books were read all together?

This chapter is trying to help you learn how to use multiplication, so it is okay to use a calculator with some of the problems.

The Magic of Multiplying
Level 1

Did you know there are 365 days in a year?

1) Daniel earned $2 helping his mom learn how to use the computer. If Daniel earned $2 every day, how much would he earn in a year?

2) Jasmine bought 12 boxes of donuts that each had 12 donuts. How many donuts did Jasmine buy?

3) Travis bought 12 mice for 59¢ each. How much did Travis spend on mice?

4) If 17 people each weigh 100 pounds, what is their total weight?

Did you know there are 16 ounces in a pound?

5) How many ounces are in 10 pounds?

The Magic of Multiplying
Level 2

1) The Weston fire department had 28 fire trucks that each had 7 hoses. How many hoses are there on all the fire trucks?

2) Isaac found that each step he took was 3 feet long. If Isaac took 1250 steps, how far did he walk?

3) Katie walked 100 yards. How many inches did Katie walk?

Did you know there are 12 inches in a foot and 3 feet in a yard?

4) A teacher collected $18.75 from each of the 27 students in her class to pay for a trip to the Field Museum. What was the total cost of the trip?

5) 8 adults, 6 children, and 4 dogs went to a drive-in movie. Tickets cost $7 for adults, $5 for children, and $3 for dogs. What was the total cost for this trip to the drive-in movie?

The Magic of Multiplying
Level 3

1) If a box of food can feed a frog for 17 days, how long will 17 boxes feed a frog?

2) The Weston Fire Department had 28 fire engines that each had 7 hoses. If each hose was 150 feet long, how many feet of hose does the fire department have?

3) There are 3 feet in a yard and 1760 yards in a mile. How many feet are in a mile?

4) How many seconds are there in a day?

5) Venus went on a picnic with her friends. She bought 7 apples for $1.25 each, 7 sandwiches for $3.75 each, and 7 desserts for $1.95 each. How much did Venus spend for her picnic?

The Magic of Multiplying
Einstein Level

1) Dale had 16 boxes. Each box had 8 rolls of copper wire that were each 60 feet long. If copper wire cost 82¢ per foot, how much are Dale's 16 boxes of wire worth?

2) There are 1000 microns in a millimeter. There are 10 millimeters in a centimeter and 10 centimeters in a decimeter. If there are 10 decimeters in a meter, how many microns are there in a meter?

3) Light travels 186,000 miles each second.
How far does light travel in a day? (24 hours)

4) Twelve people each bought 12 dozen donuts. If each donut cost 12¢, what was the total cost of all the donuts?

5) There are 4 cups in a quart and 4 quarts in a gallon. How many cups are there in 4 gallons?

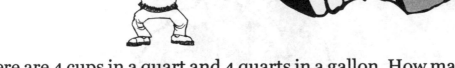

How Many Legs are There?

Emily was excited about going to the latest monster movie. As she entered the movie theatre, she saw a sign that told about a contest where the winner would receive free movie tickets for a year. The problem that needed to be solved seemed easy, but the more Emily thought about it, the more confused she got.

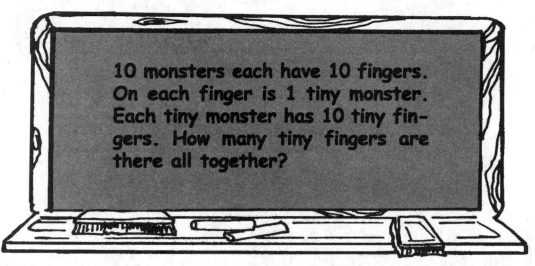

10 monsters each have 10 fingers. On each finger is 1 tiny monster. Each tiny monster has 10 tiny fingers. How many tiny fingers are there all together?

Emily finally decided to draw a picture and see if that would help her think better.

If there are 10 monsters, then they have a total of 100 fingers.

How Many Legs are There?
Level 1

1) Venus has 6 pet rats. How many legs do the rats have?

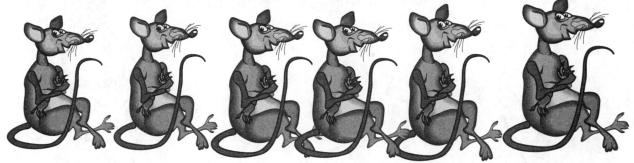

2) A farm has 55 roosters. How many legs do the roosters have?

3) Amy has a pet frog, a horse, and 8 dogs. How many legs do Amy's pets have?

4) If a barrel has 10 monkeys, how many monkey fingers are there?

5) Flies have 6 legs. If there are 50 flies on a window, how many fly legs are there?

How Many Legs are There?
Level 2

1) Nancy was giving hints to her friends to help them guess how many spiders were in her spider collection. She said that her collection had 64 legs. How many spiders does Nancy have?

Did you know that spiders have 8 legs?

2) Three spiders were sitting on a large lily pad and 4 grasshoppers were sitting on a small lily pad. Which lily pad had more legs?

Did you know that grass-hoppers are insects and all insects have 6 legs?

3) A cat, 6 kittens and a three-legged dog named Tripod are sitting on a bed. How many legs are there?

4) Claire has 8 pet ducks, 20 pigs, 6 pet spiders, 5 pet grasshoppers, and a three-legged dog named Triangle. How many legs are there? (Don't forget Claire's legs.)

5) A spider in a box had 100 babies. How many legs are there in the box?

How Many Legs are There?
Level 3

Did you know fleas have 6 legs?

1) Six dogs each had 6 puppies. All the dogs and puppies each had 6 fleas. How many legs are there?

2) Four black cats each had 4 white kittens who a year later each had 4 brown kittens. What is the total number of legs of the brown kittens?

3) There are 2 trucks that each have 2 baskets that each have 2 boxes that each hold 2 ducks. How many duck legs are there?

4) On May 1st Velvet had 1 rabbit and on May 2nd she had 2 rabbits. On May 3rd she had 4 rabbits and on May 4th she had 8 rabbits. If Velvet's rabbits keep growing in number at the same rate, on what day will she have 1024 rabbit legs?

5) Dave had 4 cats that each had 4 kittens. Dave wanted to buy shoes for all the cats and kittens. How many pairs of shoes should Dave buy?

Did you know that a pair means two?

How Many Legs are There?
Einstein Level

Remember that insects have 6 legs and that spiders have 8 legs.

1) 5 cats each had 5 kittens. The cats and kittens each had 5 fleas. Each flea had 5 tiny spiders on it. How many legs are there all together?

2) Centipedes have a lot of legs. For this problem we will pretend that each centipede has exactly 100 legs.

There are 100 trucks. In each truck there are 100 boxes. Each box has 100 centipedes. How many legs are there?

3) There are pigs and ducks on a farm. There are a total of 30 animals and 100 legs on the farm. How many ducks are there?

4) Six farmers each have 6 barrels. In each barrel are 6 cats who each have 6 kittens. How many legs are there? (Don't forget the farmer's legs.)

5) A dozen farmers each have a dozen chickens who each laid a dozen eggs. If the farmers received 12¢ for each egg, how many pennies did they get for all the eggs?

Chapter Nine

Percent Machines

When Nicky walked into the science store, he wondered if he really had saved enough money to buy a fancy microscope. The microscope cost $100, but Nicky forgot that he would have to pay sales tax. He only brought $106 to the store, so he hoped the extra $6 would be enough to pay for the sales tax.

Could you show me how to find 5% of $100?

To find percents, all you have to do is put things into the percent machine.

Percent Machine

The percent machine cuts everything into 100 equal pieces.

Percent Machines
Level 1

1) Mark had 20 pounds of rat food. He gave 25% of it to his pet rat. How many pounds did he give to his pet rat?

2) A lion ate 50% of a 500 pound deer. How many pounds did the lion eat?

3) A baby Kangaroo hopped 10% of the distance his mother hopped. If the mother hopped 10 feet, how far did the baby kangaroo hop?

4) Noah's father said that he would pay 75% of the cost of a horse. If the horse cost $1000, what would Noah's father pay?

5) A mouse said he would sell his cheese at a price that was 50% off the normal price of $70. What price is the mouse charging for his cheese?

Percent Machines
Level 2

1) The sales tax in Wormly's town is 6%. If Wormly bought a $50 coat, how much would he pay in sales tax?

2) What is 100% of $8642.31?

3) What fraction is the same as 75%?

4) What is 1% of one dollar?

5) Sammy has the same amount of money as his brother. Sammy has _____% of his brother's money.

Percent Machines
Level 3

1) A pet store was going out of business and selling $400 parrots for 80% off. What is the sale price of the parrots?

2) Seth bought hockey skates that were on sale for 15% off. If the price of the skates is usually $75, what is the sale price?

3) What fraction is the same as 95%?

4) Cory had $325 in his savings account. If he spent 20% of his money, how much did he spend?

5) When people eat at restaurants, they usually leave a 15% tip. A family spent $90 at a restaurant and was trying to figure out the amount of the tip. Their daughter, who was studying percents at school, quickly determined what the tip should be. What tip should they leave? How did their daughter determine the amount of the tip so quickly?

Percent Machines
Einstein Level

1) Jill and Rick own an ostrich farm. They had to pay a $100 vet bill because one of their ostriches was sick. Jill offered to pay $\frac{1}{2}$% of the bill. What did Jill pay?

2) David has 3 times as many pet rats as Kate. Dave has _____% of the number of rats that Kate has.

3) The sales tax in Brianna's city is 6%. $190 bat houses are on sale for 45% off. What is the sale price of the bat house with tax included?

If you buy us a house, we'll catch a lot more bugs.

4) Nancy's allowance is 175% of her brother's allowance. If her brother's allowance is $12, what is Nancy's allowance?

5) Natalie wanted to buy an $880 computer. Her father said he would pay $\frac{1}{4}$% of the cost. Natalie expected her father to pay $220, but he paid much less than that. How much money did Natalie's father pay?

Chapter Ten

How Much Will I Need?

Samantha was excited about her upcoming trip to the Pacific Ocean. She wanted to swim, see redwood trees, and most of all, she wanted to go fishing in the ocean. There was only one thing that was keeping Samantha from being really happy about the trip. She was worried that she wouldn't leave her pet snake enough food for the 24 days she would be gone.

The box of snake food that she had said that one box of food would feed 4 snakes for 3 days. This was why Samantha was confused. The directions talked about 4 snakes and she only had one snake. Then she had an idea!

If the box of food would last 3 days for 4 snakes, then the food would last 1 snake 12 days! Because Samantha was going to be away for 24 days, she would need 2 boxes of food for her pet snake.

Some problems are confusing until you think in a different way. Look at this confusing problem I wrote.

A box contained enough food to last 2 people 10 days. How long would the box feed 5 people?

Pretend that one of the people took all the food. Because the box is enough for 2 people for 10 days, it will feed one person for 20 days. Now it is easy to see that the food will last 5 people 4 days. (20 days ÷ 5 people)

1	person........20	days
2	people........10	days
5	people.........4	days

This kind of thinking is called **Think 1.** Sometimes it helps your brain to think better.

How Much Will I Need?
Level 1

1) If Jay's pet frog needs 10 flies each day, how many flies will it need for a week?

2) Meadow needs $75 for a 3 day vacation. How much would she need for a 1 day vacation?

3) If a fox eats 5 chickens each week, how many chickens will it eat in 6 weeks?

4) Dave is supposed to drink 24 ounces of water a day. How many cups is that?

Did you know that there are 8 ounces in a cup?

5) Joy's dad bought enough milk to last 4 people 5 days. How long will this much milk last 2 people?

How Much Will I Need?
Level 2

1) Dan's pet rat eats 2 ounces of cheese each day. How many pounds of cheese will he need to leave in the rat cage if he is going on an 8 day vacation?

Did you know that there are 16 ounces in a pound?

2) If a river was rising 2 feet every hour, how long would it take to rise 1/2 foot?

3) If a box of dog food will feed 3 dogs for 5 days, how long will it feed 1 dog?

4) Ali found out that it took him 2000 steps to go 1 mile. How many steps should he take if he wants to go 1/4 mile?

5) Jill is taking $10 on a vacation. After 2 days she spent a total of $2.50. If she spends money at the same rate, how much money will Jill have after 8 days of vacation?

How Much Will I Need?
Level 3

1) Matt was trying to figure out how many cups of food he needed to leave out for his dog when his family went on a 3 week vacation. Matt knew that his dog ate $1\frac{1}{2}$ cups of food in 3 days. How much food should Matt leave out for his dog?

2) Steve can paint a fence in 4 hours. Nic also takes 4 hours to paint the fence. If they work together, how long will it take them to paint 1/2 of a fence?

Hint: What fraction of the fence will Steve paint in 1 hour?

3) If a giant carrot is enough to feed 8 children, how many giant carrots would you need for 20 children?

4) If it takes a turtle 1/2 hour to walk 100 meters, how long will it take the turtle to walk 1 kilometer?

Did you know that there are 1000 meters in a kilometer?

5) If 4 people need a total of 8 pounds of food for a 1 week hike, how many pounds of food would 3 people need for a 1 week hike?

How Much Will I Need?
Einstein Level

1) If 9 ounces of food will feed a fish for 45 days, how many days will $9\frac{1}{2}$ ounces last?

2) If 3 gallons of water are needed for an 8 mile hike, how many quarts of water are needed for a 10 mile hike?

Did you know that there are 4 quarts in a gallon?

Did you know that there are 60 minutes in 1 hour?

3) If a car is traveling at a speed of 60 miles each hour, how long will it take for the car to go 1 mile?

4) If it takes a snail 12 minutes to crawl 2 meters, how many hours would it take the snail to crawl a kilometer?

5) It takes Melissa 2 hours to paint a car. It takes Dave 4 hours to paint the car. Kate also takes 4 hours to paint the car. If they all worked together, how long will it take them to paint 1 car?

Chapter Eleven

How Tall is it?

Jordan was very nervous that a big tree in his yard would fall over and crash into his bedroom. Even though the tree was far away from Jordon's house, it was a very tall tree and when the wind would blow, the tree would tip to one side and make loud cracking sounds.

Jordan knew that if he could figure out the height of the tree, he could tell whether it would hit the house if it fell. Jordan thought for hours and hours, trying to think of a way to find out how tall the tree was.

While Jordan was standing in his yard looking at the tree, he noticed that he had a shadow and that the tree had a shadow. A big smile slowly came across Jordan's face. He discovered how to find out how tall the tree was!

Jordon knew that he was 4 feet tall and when he measured his shadow he discovered that it was 2 feet long. This meant that at this time of the day, shadows were half as long as people, trees, and other objects.

Jordan measured the tree's shadow and found that it was 50 feet long. This meant that the tree was 100 feet tall!

Now all that Jordan needed to do was measure the distance from the tree to his house. When he did, Jordan found out that the distance was 110 feet. Because the tree was only 100 feet tall, Jordan knew that even if it fell, it would not hit his house.

How Tall is it?
Level 1

1) If a 5 foot person has a shadow of 10 feet, how long of a shadow does a 100 foot tall building have?

2) Amy's propeller hat flew her to the top of a tree with a 100 foot shadow. Amy is 4 feet tall and has a shadow of 8 feet. How tall is the tree?

3) A drawing of a redwood tree had a scale that said each inch equals 50 feet of real tree. If the drawing of the tree was 4 inches high, how tall was the real redwood tree?

Scale: 1 inch = 50 feet

4) Austin is standing next to a 4 foot tall fence post. The post has a shadow of 1 foot. If Austin is 80 inches tall, how long is Austin's shadow?

5) If a model for a horse is 1 inch equals 1 foot, how tall should a model be for a $6\frac{1}{2}$ foot tall horse?

How Tall is it?
Level 2

1) Lyn was making a model of the Empire State Building. She knows that it is about 1400 feet tall. She wants her model to have 1 inch stand for each 100 feet of the Empire State Building. How tall should she build her model?

2) Alex is 4 feet tall and has a shadow that is 1 foot long. If his house has a shadow of 10 feet, how tall is his house?

3) Stacie is 5 feet tall. Early in the morning while waiting for the bus, she found that her shadow was 25 feet long. Stacie's brother is 6 feet tall. How long will his shadow be?

4) A museum had a model of an Egyptian pyramid. There was a sign on the model that said 1 inch equals 10 feet. If the model was $9\frac{1}{2}$ inches high, how tall was the real pyramid?

5) Natalie is going to make a doll house that is exactly 1/4 the size of the house she lives in. If Natalie's home is 20 feet tall, how tall should she make her doll house?

How Tall is it?
Level 3

1) Sarah had a fence post in her garden that was 3 feet tall. When she measured the fence post's shadow, she found that it was 9 feet long. A tree in Sarah's yard had a shadow of 75 feet. How tall is the tree?

2) Michael, who is 4 feet tall, had a shadow of 3 feet. Michael was standing next to a tall building that had a shadow of 60 feet. How tall is the building?

3) Kate is trying to figure out how high her rocket went when she shot it into the air. Kate, who is 3 feet tall, found that her shadow was 15 feet long at the time the rocket was launched. If the shadow of her rocket went 250 feet along the ground, how high did her rocket go?

4) Jane made a doll house that was exactly 1/10 the size of the house she lives in. If Jane's doll house is 24 inches high, how many feet tall is the house Jane lives in?

5) A museum was planning to make a toy model of a 90 foot long dinosaur. They want the scale to be 1 inch of model equals 5 feet of real dinosaur. How long should the model be?

Scale: 1 inch = 5 feet

How Tall is it?
Einstein Level

1) Ben's yardstick had a shadow of 1 foot. Kristie had a ruler that was 1 foot long. How long would the ruler's shadow be?

2) Natalie's dad was going to cut a tree down. Natalie was very worried that the tree would hit her house so she decided to use math to find out the height of the tree.

Natalie measured the shadow of a 10 foot stick and found that it was 15 feet long. The tree had a shadow of 90 feet. How tall was the tree?

 3) Janet's 24 foot tall house has a shadow of 4 feet. If Janet has a shadow of 10 inches, how many feet tall is Janet?

4) When Jack got to the top of the beanstalk, he saw an enormous giant who had a shadow of 15 feet. Jack was 5 feet tall and had a shadow of 3 feet. How tall was the giant?

5) If a 2 foot tall rat had a 1 inch shadow, how long of a shadow would a yardstick have?

Magic of Math
Making Smart Guesses

Venus needed to find out about how many apples were rotten in a truck that was filled with 1000 apples. Venus really didn't want to go through the boredom of counting all the apples, so she decided to try and think of a way to use math to save her time.

After a little thinking, Venus had an idea. She would count out 100 apples and see how many rotten apples there were. When she did, Venus found out that 7 of the 100 apples were rotten.

We are rotten to the core.

Because there were 1000 apples in the truck, Venus knew that there were 10 groups of 100 apples in the truck. Venus also knew that there were about 7 rotten apples in each group of 100 apples.

Venus could now guess that there were 70 rotten apples in the truck.

These problems are pretty easy if you ask yourself how many groups of 30 are in the box.

You can find how many groups of 30 by using your calculator.
225 ÷ 30 = 7.5

There are 7.5 groups of 30 in the box. If there are 4 rotten apples in each group, then you can predict the number of rotten apples by multiplying.

7.5 x 4 = 30 rotten apples

Magic of Math - Making Smart Guesses
Level 1

1) Evan has been getting in trouble at school about 2 times each week. Predict how many times he'll get in trouble in 5 weeks.

2) If you flip a coin 1000 times, about how many times will it end up heads?

3) A box has 1000 marbles in it that are red and green. Ted closed his eyes and picked one hundred marbles. He ended up picking 40 red marbles and 60 green marbles. How many red marbles do you think were in the box before Ted picked the 100 marbles?

4) Debra saw lightning and then it took 15 seconds for the thunder to reach her ears. How far away is the storm?

Did you know that it takes sound 5 seconds to go one mile?

5) There are 30 children in Luke's class. He asked 10 children what their favorite color was. Two children said that their favorite color was yellow. Predict how many children in Luke's class have yellow as their favorite color.

Magic of Math - Making Smart Guesses
Level 2

1) Stan bought a box of 100 apples. Stan took ten apples out of the box and found that 3 were rotten. Predict how many rotten apples are in Stan's box of 100 apples.

2) Everet can rake 3 bags of leaves in 2 hours. How many minutes will it take him to rake 1 bag of leaves?

Did you know that there are 60 minutes in an hour?

3) Noah saw lightning and then it took $2\frac{1}{2}$ seconds for the thunder to reach his ears. How far away is the storm?

4) If you decided to spin the spinner 100 times, predict how many times the pointer would land on the horse.

5) Carly earned $10 baby-sitting 1 week. If she earned the same amount of money each week for a year, how much money would Carly earn?

Did you know that there are 52 weeks in a year?

Magic of Math - Making Smart Guesses
Level 3

1) Buffy is trying to figure out how long her 18 mile bike trip will take. The first 2 miles of the trip took 20 minutes. How many hours will her 18 mile trip take?

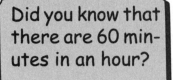

Did you know that there are 60 minutes in an hour?

2) Janet bought a bag of 1000 jelly beans. There were 3 colors in the bag. Janet was trying to guess how many of each color were in the bag so she took out 100 jelly beans and counted each color.

20 green   5 red   75 blue

How many red jelly beans do you think are in the bag of 1000 jelly beans?

3) After Ricky saw lightning, it took $7\frac{1}{2}$ seconds for the thunder to reach his ears. How far away is the storm?

4) Jose needed 90 apples for his birthday party, but every box of apples he bought had a lot of rotten apples in it. When he bought a box of 40 apples, 10 were rotten. If Jose wants 90 good apples, how many boxes of apples should he buy?

5) Ed runs 75 yards in 12 seconds. If he runs at the same speed, how much time would it take Ed to run 100 yards?

Magic of Math - Making Smart Guesses
Einstein Level

1) Brianna is 4 feet tall and her shadow is 3 feet long. Brianna's father has a shadow of 4 feet 6 inches. How tall is Brianna's father?

2) Kristie was bored one summer so she spun the spinner shown below 1200 times. How many times would you guess that the spinner landed on the A?

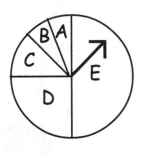

3) Megan wanted to predict how many students in her school had birthdays during the Spring. If there were 288 students in her school, how many students would you predict had birthdays during the Spring?

Did you know that each season is 3 months long?

4) Jake knew that sound takes 5 seconds to travel 1 mile. Jake stood on one side of a river and yelled at a mountain that was on the other side. Jake heard an echo 20 seconds later. How far was it from Jake to the mountain?

5) Can you think of a way to always be able to know how far away a thunderstorm is?

What are These Strange Numbers?

Ben was very upset. All the children in his family were supposed to write how much money they had on a large blackboard, but Ben didn't know what to write.

All the other children wrote amounts of money like $25 or $42, but Ben wasn't sure what to write. He had $15 in his piggy bank, but he borrowed $35 from his mother to buy a computer game.

McKenna	$42
Carly	$25
Stacie	$37
Ben	$?

Ben knew that because he owed his mother $35 and he only had $15 in his piggy bank, the amount of money he had was less than $0. But how could he write that amount of money?

You owe me $35!

What Ben needs to learn about are negative numbers. If he combines his money in the piggy bank with what he owes his mother, he ends up with a minus $20.

$15

+

-$35

Answer -$20

Negative numbers are used to show things that are less than 0. This submarine is 400 feet below the surface of the ocean, so we say it is at -400 feet.

What are These Strange Numbers?
Level 1

1) Anna has $5 in her purse, but she owes her mom $6. How much money would you say that Anna has?

2) Tom has $20 in his savings account, but he owes his dad $20. How much money would you say that Tom has?

3) If the temperature starts at -5° and drops to -10°, how many degrees did it drop?

4) Stu has $10 in his piggy bank, but he owes his sister $15. How much money would you say that Stu has?

5) Nancy owed her mother $10 and she owed her brother $10. How much money would you say that Nancy has?

a) $20
b) -$20
c) $0

What are These Strange Numbers?
Level 2

1) Lyn had $25 in her pocket, but she owed her mom $35. How much money would you say Lyn had?

2) 20 - 15 is an easy problem, the answer is 5. What is the answer to the problem 15 - 20?

3) If the temperature is 10°F and then gets 15° colder, what is the new temperature?

4) Four brothers had no money and they each owed their dad $5. How much money do the four brothers have all together?

5) The highest point on Earth is 6 miles above sea level. The lowest point is a spot in the ocean that is about 7 miles deep. If a worm is at the lowest point, how much higher than the worm is a mountain climber who is at the highest point on Earth?

What are These Strange Numbers?
Level 3

1) Three friends decided to combine all their money. Rachel has $17, Lauri has $3 and Luke owes his mom $11. How much money would you say they have all together?

2) The temperature was 8 degrees below zero in the morning and then rose to 12 degrees above zero at lunchtime. How many degrees did the temperature rise?

3) Jill received $15 for her birthday. She spent $12 and then found $7 on the sidewalk. On her way home she lost $9.50. How much money does Jill have now?

4) Scott had no money, so he borrowed $11 from Dan. He also borrowed $7 from his dad. After he spent the money he borrowed, Scott found $10. How much money would you say Scott has now?

5) One day the temperature at a science camp in Antarctica was -120°F. That same day, the temperature at the Panama canal was 100°F. How many degrees warmer was it at the Panama Canal than at the science camp?

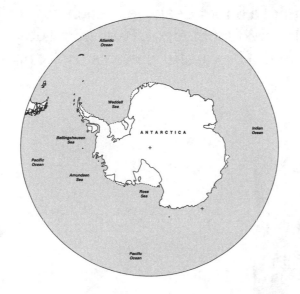

What are These Strange Numbers?
Einstein Level

1) Samantha had $8, but she owed $17 to her grandmother. For Samantha's birthday, her grandmother gave her $5 and also wrote the following on a birthday card:

In addition to the $5 present, I am also taking away $10 of the debt that you owe me.

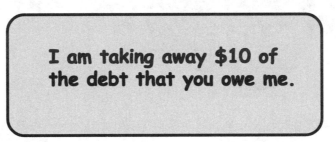

I am taking away $10 of the debt that you owe me.

How much money would you say that Samantha has now?

2) A snake was at the bottom of a 6 foot deep well. Each day it would climb up 5 feet, but then it would slip down 4 feet at night. How many days would it take for the snake to get out of the well? (Be careful, this is a tricky problem.)

3) The lowest possible temperature is -459.6°F. Water boils at 212°F. If the temperature dropped from 212°F to -459.6°F, how many degrees did it drop?

4) Two clocks start at noon. One clock is broken and loses 10 minutes every hour. When the good clock says 12:00 midnight, what time will the broken clock say?

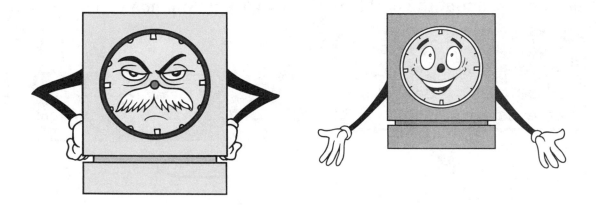

5) If the temperature is 10°F and the wind is blowing at 30 miles per hour, the temperature feels like it is -33°F. How much colder does a child feel who is out in the wind when you compare him to one who is outside and not in the wind?

Chapter Fourteen

Let's Share

Amanda wanted to split $40.28 with her brother, but she was having a hard time trying to decide how to do it mentally. She knew that it would be easy to do if she only had $40. She also knew it would be easy to do if she had only 40¢ or if she only had 8¢.

After thinking about the problem for a long time, Amanda had a brilliant idea.

If I break $40.28 into dollars, dimes and pennies, it will be easy to divide into two equal amounts.

That was a great idea! I am going to try to do division problems mentally if I can.

Let's Share
Level 1

1) Ben and Amy found $3 on the sidewalk. If they want to split the money evenly, how much will they each get?

2) If a television program starts at 5:00 and ends at 6:00, when is it half over?

3) Three friends earned a total of $60 raking leaves. If they split the money evenly, how much money will each person get?

4) If 10 pencils cost $1.00, how much does 1 pencil cost?

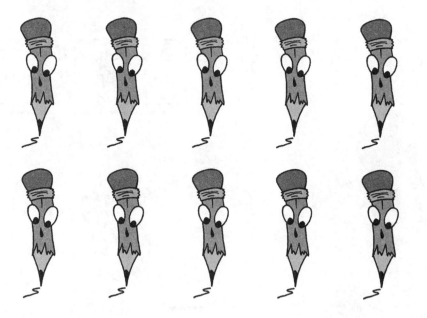

5) Three children decided to save money so they could buy a present for their mom. If the present cost $75, how much money should each child save?

Let's Share
Level 2

1) Four friends are planning to share a two pound ginger bread boy. How many ounces of cookie will each friend receive?

Did you know that there are 16 ounces in a pound?

2) Three brothers decided to share the cost of a pet turtle. If the turtle cost $21.75, how much money should each brother pay?

3) A family of 4 is going on a 10 mile hike. They have a very heavy backpack that they are going to take turns carrying. If they want to be fair, how many miles should each member of the family carry the backpack?

4) If a bag containing 1000 jelly beans is going to be shared by 50 people, how many jelly beans will each person get?

5) If a movie starts at 4:00 and ends at 7:00, at what time is it half over?

Let's Share
Level 3

1) Eight children took a 2 gallon container with them when they went on a hike in the Grand Canyon. If they shared equally, how many cups of water will they each be able to drink?

Did you know that there are 4 quarts in a gallon, 2 pints in a quart and 2 cups in each pint?

2) It took Deva 3 minutes to solve the number cube game. If Dan can solve the game in half the time, how many seconds does it take Dan to solve the number cube game?

3) Steve and his 2 sisters bought an ant farm. If they agreed to split the $24.90 cost of the ant farm, how much is Steve's share of the cost?

4) A loaf of French bread is 18 inches long. If 8 people are splitting the loaf, how long a piece will each person get?

5) If 12 dozen donuts cost $36.00, how much does 1 donut cost?

Let's Share
Einstein Level

1) Three friends opened a lemonade stand and decided to keep it open 5 hours each day. How long should each person work at the lemonade stand each day if the 3 friends are going to share the 5 hours of work?

2) Because she has diabetes, Erin has to take 1/4 ounce of a certain medicine each day. If her mom bought a gallon of the medicine, how many days will the medicine last?

Did you know that there are 4 quarts in a gallon, 2 pints in a quart, 2 cups in each pint and 8 ounces in a cup?

3) A 1/4 pound of broccoli is to be shared by 3 sisters. If they share it equally, what fraction of a pound will each sister receive?

4) A movie starts at 5:30 and goes until 8:00. At what time will the movie be 1/3 over?

5) Sammy found a bag of money. He decided to give 1/2 the money to his best friend, 1/4 of the money to his sister, 1/8 of the money to his mother and 1/16 of the money to his dad. The amount of money that was left was $5. How much money was in the bag when Sammy found it?

How Far Away is it?

Stacy rides to school with her dad every morning. It takes her 1/2 hour to get to school and her dad drives at a speed of 60 miles per hour. Stacy often wonders how far away her school is, but she hasn't been able to figure it out.

As you can see, if you know the time and the speed, it is easy to find the distance. Before you start thinking about buying a distance machine, I want you to look inside of the machine.

All the machine does is multiply! I guess it would be a waste of money to buy a distance machine.

Try the problems on the next page. Remember that you can find the distance by multiplying the speed by the time.

Speed x Time

How Far Away is it?
Level 1

1) Mr. Burns walked for 5 hours at a speed of 2 miles per hour. How far did Mr. Burns travel?

2) A mosquito flew at a speed of 1 mile per hour for $2\frac{1}{2}$ hours. How far did the mosquito fly?

3) A dinosaur was running at a speed of 20 miles per hour. If it went at that speed for 4 hours, how far did it run?

4) If a turtle moved at a speed of 1/2 mile per hour, how far would it go in 4 hours?

5) If a roach crawled at a speed of 5 feet per minute, how far would it go in 3 minutes?

How Far Away is it?
Level 2

1) It took Micah 5 hours to finish a 30 mile bike trip. What speed did he travel at?

2) If you walked at a speed of 3 miles per hour, how long would it take you to walk 18 miles?

3) How long does it take for the sound of the caveman's voice to travel 1/2 mile?

4) Stan can walk his dog 4 miles in an hour. If it takes Stan 30 minutes to walk his dog to the park, how far away is the park?

5) When Seth runs from his home to school, his speed is 4 miles per hour. If it took Seth 15 minutes to get to school, how far away is Seth's school?

How Far Away is it?
Level 3

1) It takes sound 5 seconds to travel one mile. How far does sound travel in 100 seconds?

2) Nancy is always complaining about how long it takes to get to her grandmother's house. Her family drives at a speed of 60 miles per hour and it takes 2 hours and 20 minutes to get to her grandmother's house. How far away does her grandmother live?

3) Rachel was riding her skateboard at a speed of 15 miles per hour. If her trip to the post office took 20 minutes, how far away is the post office?

4) You need to be at your cousin's house at noon. If the distance you need to travel is 200 miles and you travel at a speed of 50 miles per hour, what time should you leave your house?

5) Light travels at a speed of 186,000 miles each second. How far does light travel in 1 minute? (Use your calculator.)

How Far Away is it?
Einstein Level

1) If you are traveling at 60 miles per hour, how far do you travel in 1 minute?

2) If you hear thunder $12\frac{1}{2}$ seconds after you see lightning, how far away is the storm?

Remember that it takes sound 5 seconds to travel one mile.

3) If you run a mile in 6 minutes, what speed are you running at?

4) It took Dan 12 minutes to go a mile in his wheelchair. How fast was Dan moving?

5) During a thunderstorm, it took $27\frac{1}{2}$ seconds for the thunder to reach McKenna's ears after she saw the lightning. How far away is the storm?

When are We Going to Get There?

When are We Going to Get There?
Level 1

1) A hippo went on a trip at a speed of 3 miles per hour. If the distance it traveled was 15 miles, how long did the trip take?

2) A lion was chasing a deer at a speed of 20 miles per hour. If the lion went 10 miles, how long did the chase last?

a) 1 hour
b) 2 hours
c) 1/2 hour

3) If it takes a kangaroo 3 hours to travel 15 miles, how long will it take the kangaroo to travel 20 miles?

4) The Easter Bunny went on a 250 mile trip at a speed of 50 miles per hour. If he left at noon, what time will his trip end?

5) A duck was flying south for the winter at a speed of 5 miles per hour. How long will it take it to travel 100 miles?

When are We Going to Get There?
Level 2

1) Ricky the rat traveled 20 miles at a speed of 2 miles per hour. How long did the trip take?

2) If a whale swims at a speed of 45 miles per hour, how long will it take to swim 180 miles?

3) How long would a 60 mile bike trip take if your speed was 12 miles per hour?

4) Natalie is going on a vacation to visit the Smoky Mountains. Her family will travel at a speed of 50 miles per hour. If the Smoky Mountains are 400 miles from her home, how long will it take Natalie to get to the Smoky Mountains?

5) The distance from one end of the United States to the other end is 3000 miles. If you traveled on a plane that went 500 miles per hour, how long would your trip take?

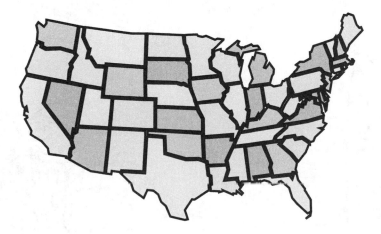

When are We Going to Get There?
Level 3

1) Renee rode her skates 8 miles to school at a speed of 16 miles per hour. How long did it take Renee to get to school?

2) Stan left home at 8:00 for a 25 mile hike. If Stan walks at a speed of 2.5 miles per hour, what time will he finish the hike?

3) When astronauts travel the 250,000 miles to the moon, their speed averages about 3125 miles per hour. How many hours does it take to get to the moon?

4) Dave and his sister took a 26 mile bike trip. If they travel at a speed of 10.4 miles per hour, how long will the trip take them? (Use a calculator.)

5) Mariah's grandfather lives 175 miles away. If she travels at a speed of 50 miles per hour, how long will it take Mariah to get to her grandmother's house?

When are We Going to Get There?
Einstein Level

1) A tortoise and a hare had a famous race. If the race was 5 miles and the tortoise went at a speed of 1/4 mile per hour, how long did it take the tortoise to finish the race?

2) A fox started running at noon and ran 1 mile. If it ran at a speed of 5 miles per hour, at what time did it finish its run?

3) Sam the snail crawled 1/4 mile at a speed of 1/10 mile per hour. How long did it take Sam the snail?

4) A Cheetah can run at a speed of 70 miles per hour for only short distances because it gets tired. If a cheetah could run 17.5 miles at 70 miles per hour, how long would it take? (We are just pretending because a cheetah cannot run at 70 miles per hour for that distance.)

5) Some fighter jets can travel at speeds of 800 miles per hour. At that speed, how long would it take a fighter jet to travel 160 miles?

Chapter Seventeen

What is My Speed?

I wish my wheelchair had a speedometer so I could tell how fast I was going.

I have a speed machine that will tell you how fast you are traveling. Look at this problem and watch how the speed machine easily solves it.

Jason rode his wheelchair in a marathon that was 25 miles long. It took Jason 5 hours to finish the race. What was Jason's average speed?

On the next page you will see that I am going to put the distance and the time into the machine. After a minute or so the speed will come out.

Speed Machine

Those problems are easy for the machine. All you need to do is put your time in and your distance in. The machine will then give you the speed.

Make sure that your time is always in hours and your distance is in miles. In this problem, your time is 1/4 hour.

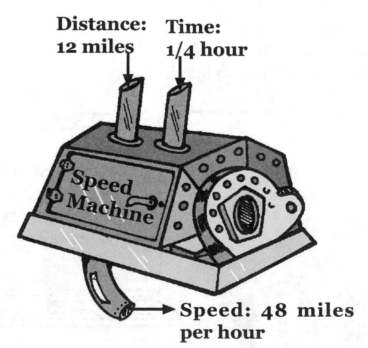

Distance: 12 miles

Time: 1/4 hour

Speed: 48 miles per hour

So, if I walk 15 miles and it takes me 3 hours, I just do 15 ÷ 3 = 5 miles per hour?

Distance: **Time:**
15 miles   **3 hours**

Speed:
5 miles
per hour

All you need to do is take the distance and divide it by the time. That will give you your speed.

Now it is obvious that you don't need the machine. You can just use your brain or a calculator.

What is My Speed?
Level 1

1) If Ashton walked 10 miles in 2 hours, what was his speed?

2) It took Jose 3 hours to drive to college. If the college is 90 miles away, what was Jose's average speed?

3) A family went on a 5 mile hike. If it took them 2 hours, what was their speed?

4) A mosquito flew 1 mile across a lake in 10 minutes. How fast did the mosquito fly?

5) If it takes supermouse 30 minutes to fly 7 miles, how fast is he flying?

What is My Speed?
Level 2

1) A falcon flew 40 miles in 20 minutes. What was its speed?

2) If a whale swims 144 miles in 12 hours, what is its speed?

3) If an eagle flew 150 miles in 6 hours, what was its speed?

4) Emily went to New Orleans on vacation. If the distance she traveled was 600 miles and it took her 20 hours, what was her average speed?

5) The distance from one end of the United States to the other end is 3000 miles. If you wanted to cross the United States in 15 hours, what speed would you have to travel at?

What is My Speed?
Level 3

1) A boy was mad that he had to go home from the playground, so he walked very slowly. If it took him 5 hours to walk 1 mile, what was his speed in miles per hour?

2) If a man ran 1/5 of a mile in 12 minutes, what was his speed in miles per hour?

3) If it took a spacecraft 12 hours to travel 48,000 miles, what was its speed?

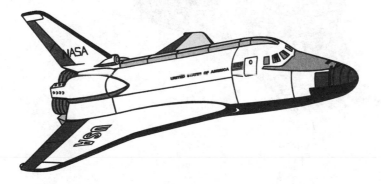

4) Roger the rat traveled one mile in 6 minutes. How fast was the canoe traveling?

5) A train that was 2 miles long took 15 minutes to travel by a railroad crossing. At what speed was the train moving?

What is My Speed?
Einstein Level

1) It takes sound 5 seconds to travel 1 mile. What is its speed in miles per hour?

2) Light travels 186,000 miles per second. What is the speed of light in miles per hour?

3) If a car is traveling 1 mile each minute, how fast is it traveling?

4) If the space shuttle orbits the Earth in $1\frac{1}{2}$ hours and travels 27,000 miles in one orbit, how fast is the space shuttle traveling?

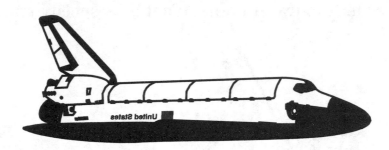

5) The lunar rover was a vehicle that astronauts brought to the moon. If it took 8 minutes to drive the lunar rover 1 mile, what was its speed?

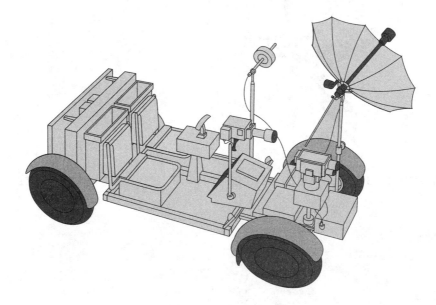

How Much Does it Weigh?

Sometimes it can be very important to know how much things weigh. If a car has a weight limit of 1000 pounds and you are putting boxes of books in the car, it is easy to overload the car and damage it.

Serious accidents can happen if you don't pay attention to weight limits. A famous singer named Aaliyah died in a plane crash because the weight limit of the plane was ignored.

Make sure you know how to find the weight of things. I didn't know this metal block weighed so much and it broke a board and fell on me.

How Much Does it Weigh?
Level 1

1) If an elephant weighs 2 tons, how many pounds does it weigh?

Remember that there are 16 ounces in each pound and there are 2000 pounds in each ton.

2) Andy has 8 ounces of chocolate. How many pounds does he have?

3) A small bus weighs 5000 pounds. How many tons is the bus?

4) Bill weighs half as much as his dad. Bill's dog Shadow weighs half as much as Bill weighs. If Bill's dad weighs 120 pounds, how much does Shadow weigh?

5) If apples cost $4 for each pound, how much does $1 worth of apples weigh?

How Much Does it Weigh?
Level 2

1) A 5 ton block of ice was put out in the sun at noon. If it loses half its weight every hour, what will it weigh at 4:00 in the afternoon?

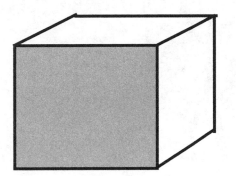

2) If 15 pounds are added to a brick, its weight is the same as 3 bricks. How much does 1 brick weigh?

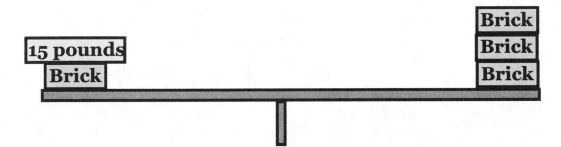

3) If chocolate covered peanuts cost $6 per pound, what is the weight of $1.50 worth of peanuts?

4) If a board that is a yard long weighs 12 pounds, how much does 1/2 foot of the board weigh?

5) Nancy's mom weighs twice as much as Nancy. Nancy's mom weighs 3 times as much as Larry. If Nancy weighs 60 pounds, how much does Larry weigh?

How Much Does it Weigh?
Level 3

1) If 5 bricks weigh 80 pounds, what do $2\frac{1}{4}$ bricks weigh?

2) A magic frog loses half its weight every day. If the magic frog weighs 6 pounds on Monday, how many ounces does it weigh on Friday?

3) Will the magic frog in problem #2 ever weigh zero pounds?

4) If a 1000 pound hibernating bear lost 15% of its weight over the winter, how much will it weigh when spring starts?

5) If $3\frac{1}{2}$ gold bars weigh 49 pounds, how much will 4 gold bars weigh?

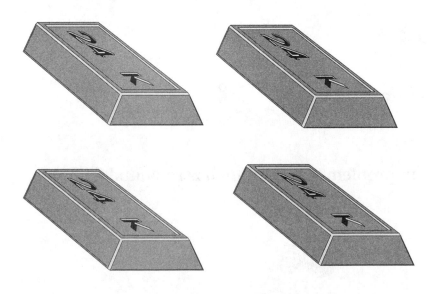

How Much Does it Weigh?
Einstein Level

1) If a gallon of a certain liquid weighs 24 pounds, what does 1/2 cup of the liquid weigh?

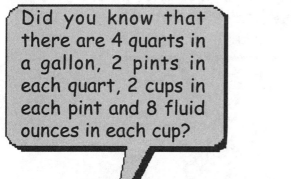

Did you know that there are 4 quarts in a gallon, 2 pints in each quart, 2 cups in each pint and 8 fluid ounces in each cup?

2) If a 1 inch by 1 inch piece of cardboard weighs 1 ounce, how much does a 1 foot by 1 foot piece of cardboard weigh?

3) If a gallon of milk weighs 16 pounds, how many ounces does a fluid ounce of milk weigh?

4) If a decimeter of rope weighs 3.9 ounces, how much does an inch of rope weigh?

Did you know that there are 10 decimeters in a meter and that there are about 39 inches in a meter?

5) If a dozen donuts weighs 3 pounds, how many ounces does 1/4 of a donut weigh?

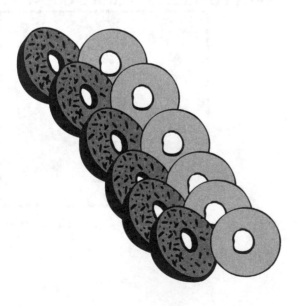

Changing Machines

Jose had a problem. He just received his drivers license and he wanted to make sure that he didn't speed when he drove, but his speedometer only told him how fast he was traveling in miles per hour. This wouldn't normally be a problem, but Jose was going to take a trip to Canada.

Canadians do not measure distances in miles like people in the United States do. Canada, like almost all other countries, uses the metric system. The metric system measures long distances in kilometers, not miles.

This was the reason that Jose had a problem. The signs in Canada said that the speed limit was 90 kilometers per hour.

If Jose could only find a way to change kilometers into miles, then he could tell what the speed limit was in miles per hour.

I have some machines that Jose can use to help him. They are called changing machines. Look at the kilometer to miles changing machine.

Kilometers to Miles

90 Kilometers

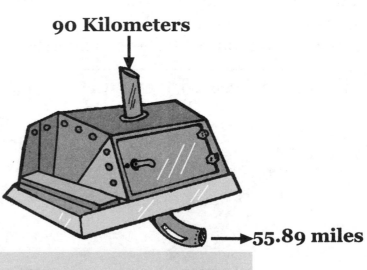

55.89 miles

Kilometers to Miles

I see how the machine works. You put in the kilometers, and the machine changes it into miles.

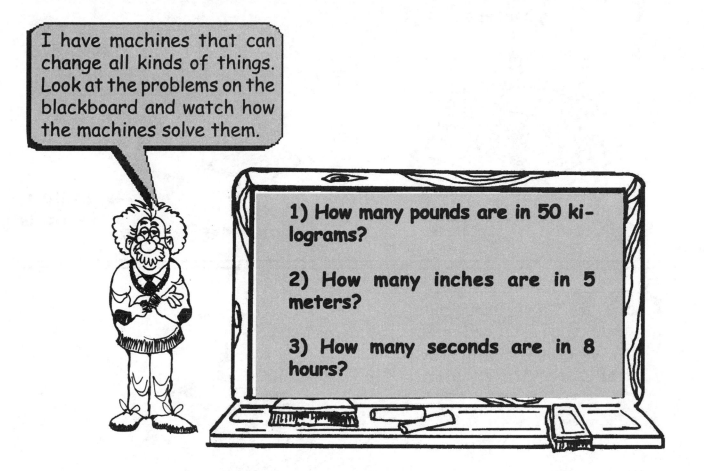

I have machines that can change all kinds of things. Look at the problems on the blackboard and watch how the machines solve them.

1) How many pounds are in 50 kilograms?

2) How many inches are in 5 meters?

3) How many seconds are in 8 hours?

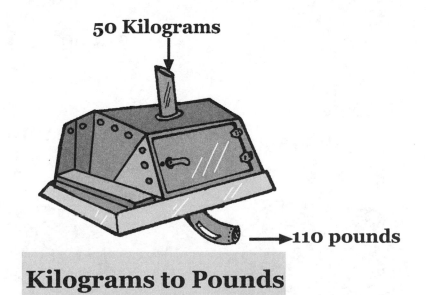

50 Kilograms

110 pounds

Kilograms to Pounds

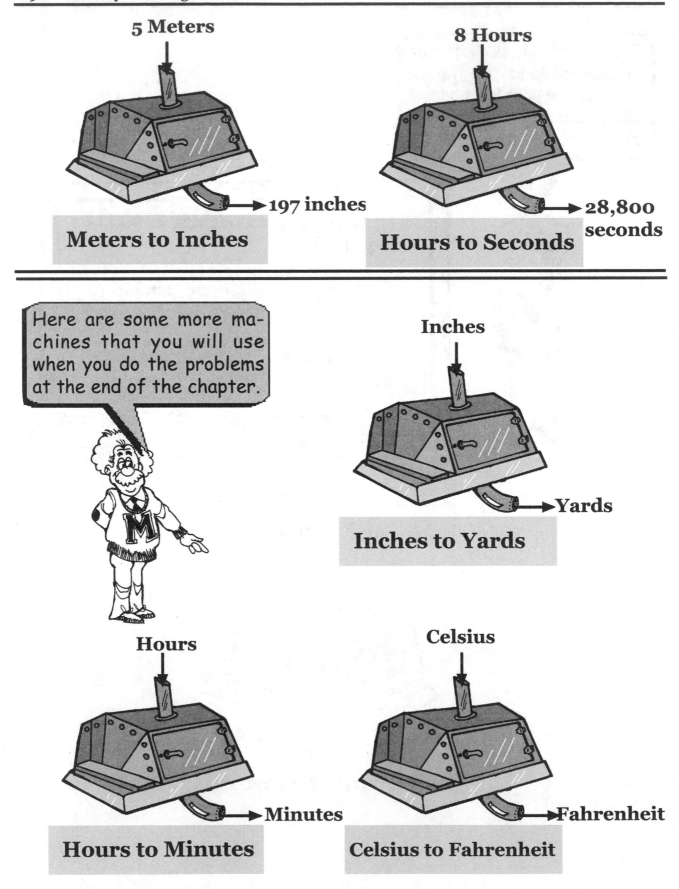

5 Meters

→ **197 inches**

Meters to Inches

8 Hours

→ **28,800 seconds**

Hours to Seconds

Here are some more machines that you will use when you do the problems at the end of the chapter.

Inches

→ **Yards**

Inches to Yards

Hours

→ **Minutes**

Hours to Minutes

Celsius

→ **Fahrenheit**

Celsius to Fahrenheit

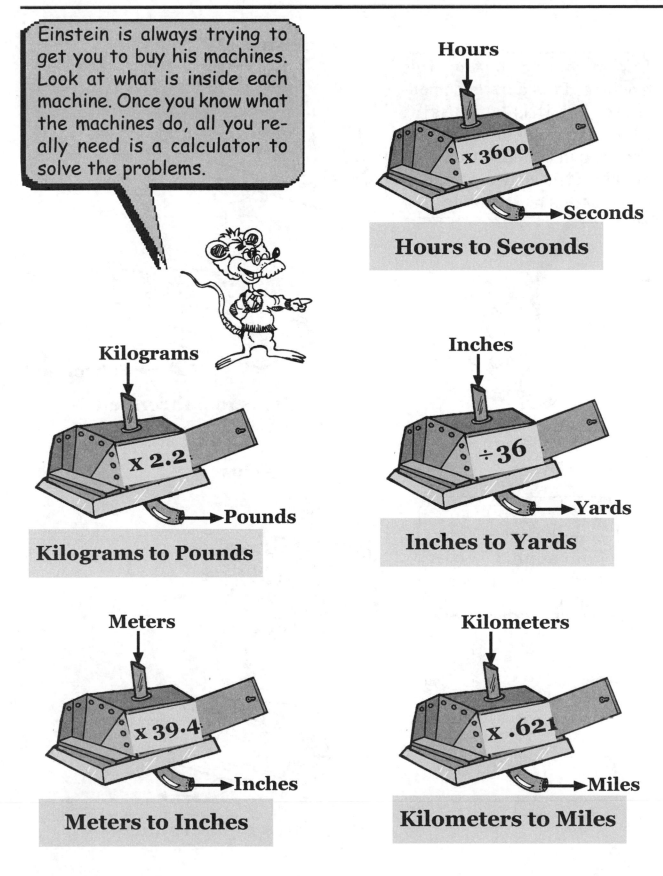

Einstein is always trying to get you to buy his machines. Look at what is inside each machine. Once you know what the machines do, all you really need is a calculator to solve the problems.

Hours

x 3600

Seconds

Hours to Seconds

Kilograms

x 2.2

Pounds

Kilograms to Pounds

Inches

÷36

Yards

Inches to Yards

Meters

x 39.4

Inches

Meters to Inches

Kilometers

x .621

Miles

Kilometers to Miles

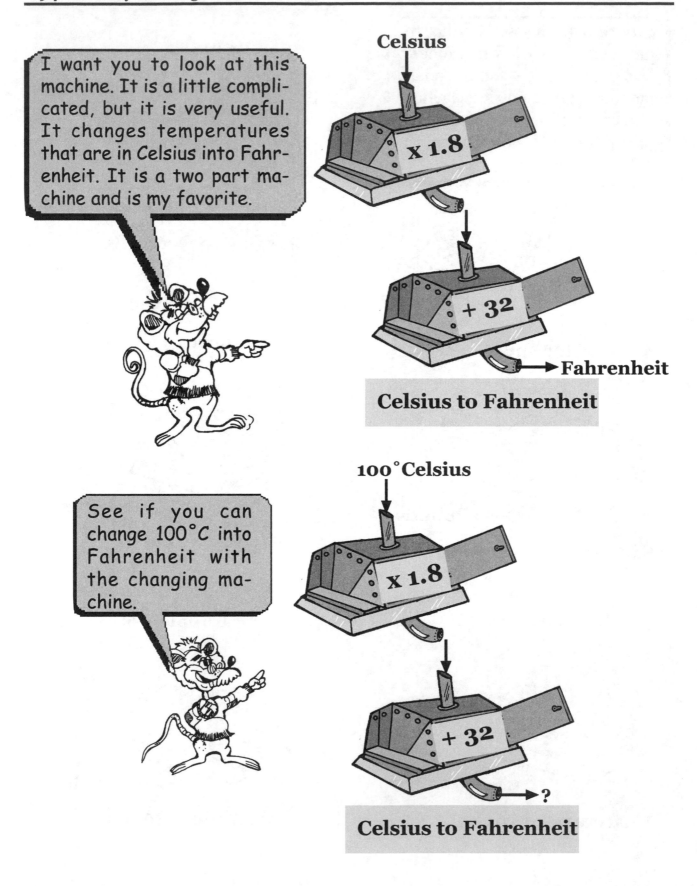

Celsius

x 1.8

+ 32

Fahrenheit

Celsius to Fahrenheit

I want you to look at this machine. It is a little complicated, but it is very useful. It changes temperatures that are in Celsius into Fahrenheit. It is a two part machine and is my favorite.

See if you can change 100°C into Fahrenheit with the changing machine.

100°Celsius

x 1.8

+ 32

?

Celsius to Fahrenheit

Before you start to do problems with the machines, there is something very important that you must know.

Some problems force you to go through the machines in reverse. When you do this, do the opposite operation.

Suppose you are asked to find out how many inches are in 8 yards. This problem forces you to go through the changing machine in reverse. Because you are going in reverse, change division to multiplication.

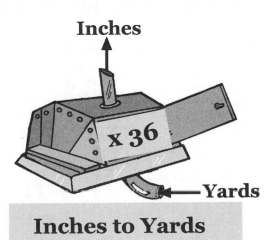

Inches

x 36

Yards

Inches to Yards

Changing Machines
Level 1

1) Leon is from France so he gives his weight in kilograms. If Leon weighs 50 kilograms, how many pounds does he weigh?

2) How many hours are in 600 minutes?

3) How many inches are in 10 meters?

4) How many yards are in 72 inches?

5) Which is longer, a mile or a kilometer?

Changing Machines
Level 2

1) Eric was visiting Germany and called home and said that the temperature was 40° C. Eric's dad was trying to figure out whether Eric was hot or cold. Is 40°C a hot or cold temperature?

2) How many hours are in 18,000 seconds?

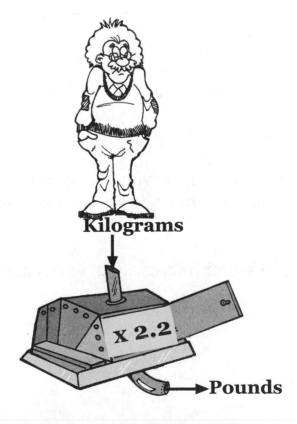

3) How many inches are in 1/2 meter?

4) How many inches are in 10 yards?

5) If Einstein weighs 176 pounds, how many kilograms does he weigh?

Kilograms to Pounds

Changing Machines
Level 3

1) If a moose ran 1000 meters, how many feet did the moose run?

2) Water boils at 100°C. If you used the Fahrenheit scale, at what temperature would water boil?

3) Walter is driving at a speed of 100 kilometers per hour. The speed limit is 65 miles per hour. Is Walter speeding?

4) Water freezes at 32°F. What is this in Celsius?

5) How many meters are in 10 feet? (Round to the nearest whole meter.)

Changing Machines
Einstein Level

Did you know that there are 5280 feet in one mile?

1) If Davis walked 10,000 meters, how many miles did he walk? (Round to the nearest mile.)

2) In the summer, temperatures can reach 100°F. What is 100°F in Celsius? (Round to the nearest whole degree.)

3) Megan is visiting the United States. Her car's speedometer only gives the speed in kilometers per hour. If the speed limit is 55 miles per hour, how many kilometers per hour can Megan drive? (Round to the nearest whole number.)

4) The normal body temperature is 98.6°F. Debra was baby-sitting and all she could find was a Celsius thermometer. When she takes the temperature of a sick baby, what should the thermometer read if the baby's temperature is normal?

5) If you put n hours through the hours to seconds machine, what will come out the other end?

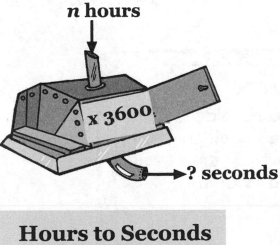

n **hours**

x 3600

? seconds

Hours to Seconds

I Know a Math Language

Algebra is scary to some children because it is a kind of math that usually isn't done until students are older and it looks like it is hard. But algebra really isn't that difficult if you remember that it is a math language.

If you go to France, you have to change English words into French words.

Algebra is just like that. When you have a problem, you need to change the problem into algebra. I think it is kind of fun.

Look at this problem. I am going to turn it into the language of algebra. We won't worry about solving it now, we'll learn that in the next chapter. In this chapter, you will learn how to change problems into algebra.

Rachel is three years older than Dan. Luke is six years older than Dan. If you add up their ages, you will get 57. How old is Dan?

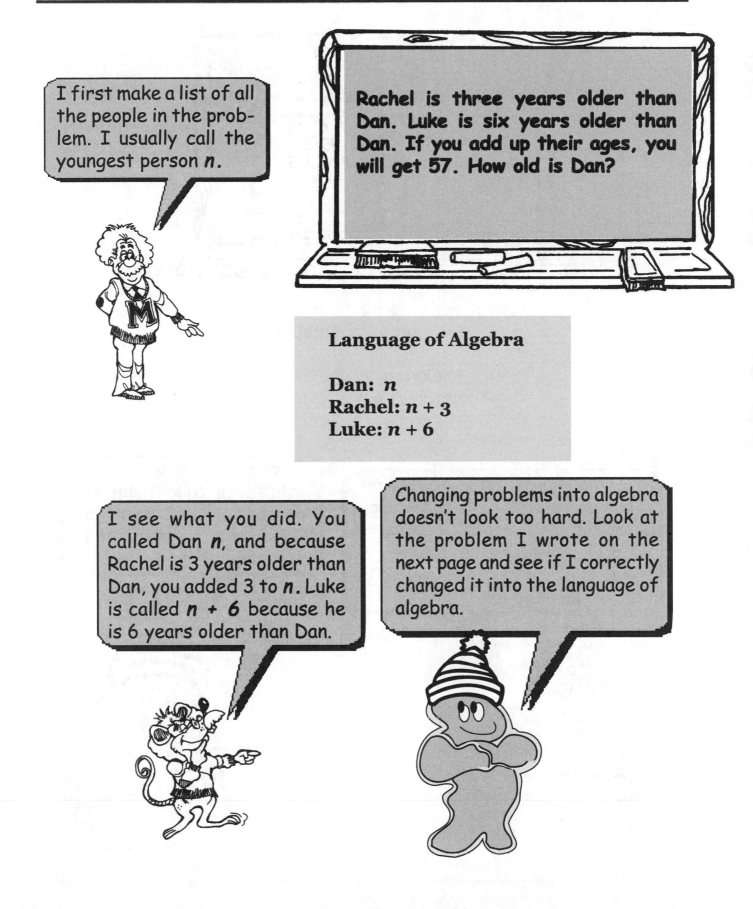

I first make a list of all the people in the problem. I usually call the youngest person *n*.

Rachel is three years older than Dan. Luke is six years older than Dan. If you add up their ages, you will get 57. How old is Dan?

Language of Algebra

Dan: *n*
Rachel: *n* + 3
Luke: *n* + 6

I see what you did. You called Dan *n*, and because Rachel is 3 years older than Dan, you added 3 to *n*. Luke is called *n* + 6 because he is 6 years older than Dan.

Changing problems into algebra doesn't look too hard. Look at the problem I wrote on the next page and see if I correctly changed it into the language of algebra.

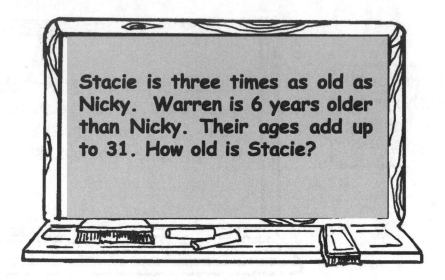

Stacie is three times as old as Nicky. Warren is 6 years older than Nicky. Their ages add up to 31. How old is Stacie?

Language of Algebra

Nicky: *n*
Stacie: *3n*
Warren: *n + 6*

You did it perfectly. You called Nicky *n* because he is the youngest. Warren is *n + 6* because he is 6 years older than Nicky and Stacie is *3n* because she is 3 times Nicky's age.

I love turning problems into the math language of algebra. Now I want to learn how to write and solve equations!

I Know a Math Language
Level 1

1) Jackie has 6 more apples than Dave. If you call the number of apples that Dave has *n*, what would you call the numbers of apples that Jackie has in the math language of algebra?

Dave: *n*
Jackie:

2) Brianna's brother is 9 years older than her. Brianna also has a sister who is one year older than her. If you call Brianna *n*, what do you call her brother and sister in the math language of algebra?

Brianna: *n*
Brother:
Sister:

3) Dave is 6 inches shorter than his dad. If you call his dad *n*, what do you call Dave in the math language of algebra?

Dad: *n*
Dave:

4) Venus is twice as old as her brother. If you call her brother n, what do you call Venus in the math language of algebra?

Brother: n
Venus:

5) In a pet store, cats cost three times as much as rabbits and dogs cost $20 more than rabbits. If you call the cost of each rabbit n, what do you call the cost of one cat and one dog in the math language of algebra?

Rabbit: n
Cat:
Dog:

I Know a Math Language
Level 2

1) Emily is twice as old as Mel, who is three years older than Nancy. If Nancy is called n, what are Emily and Mel called in the math language of algebra?

Nancy: n
Mel:
Emily:

2) Bill weighs 42 pounds more than Steve and Steve's weight is three times what his pet dog weighs. If the dog is n, what do you call Bill and Steve in the math language of algebra?

Dog: n
Bill:
Steve:

3) If Anita walked for n hours, how many minutes did she walk?

Hours: n
Minutes:

Did you know that there are 60 minutes in an hour?

4) Devon walked for *n* yards. How many inches did Devon walk?

Yards: *n*
Inches:

Did you know that there are 36 inches in a yard?

5) Stuart ran an unknown number of miles that we will call *n*. Write how many feet Stuart ran using the math language of algebra.

Miles: *n*
Feet:

Did you know that there are 5280 feet in each mile?

I Know a Math Language
Level 3

1) Mike threw a baseball an unknown number of feet we'll call *n*. Mike was asked how far he threw his baseball in yards. Using the math language of algebra, how far did Mike throw his baseball in yards?

Feet: *n*
Yards:

2) There are *n* quarters in a pile. The value of one quarter is 25 cents and the value of two quarters is 50 cents. What is the value of *n* quarters?

Value of *n* quarters:

3) A farm has *n* horses, 20 pigs, and a three-legged dog named Tripod. Use the math language of algebra to tell how many legs there are on the farm.

Horse legs:
Pig legs:
Tripod:

Total:

4) There are *n* gallons of water in the bathtub. Put the following measurements into the math language of algebra:

Gallons: *n*
Quarts:
Pints:
Cups:

Did you know that there are 2 cups in a pint, 2 pints in a quart and 4 quarts in a gallon?

5) There are *n* nickels in a pile. The value of one nickel is 5 cents. The value of two nickels is 10 cents. What is the value of *n* nickels?

Value of *n* nickels:

I Know a Math Language
Einstein Level

1) Rick rode his toy car for *n* minutes. How many hours would you say he rode his toy car?

Minutes: *n*
Hours:

2) There are only pigs and cows on a farm. There are 75 total animals and the cows are called *n*. What do you call the number of pigs using the math language of algebra?

Cows: *n*
Pigs:

3) Tom's age is double his brother Sam's age. Jordan is 6 years older than Sam and Laura is 1/2 of Tom's age. Sam is also three times older than his pet rat named Shadow. Write all their ages in the math language of algebra. Call Sam's age *n*.

Sam: *n*
Tom:
Jordan:
Laura:
Shadow:

4) If you call a meter n, use the math language of algebra to write what you would call a decimeter, centimeter, millimeter and a micron.

Meter: n
Decimeter:
Centimeter:
Millimeter:
Micron:

Did you know that there are 10 decimeters in a meter, 10 centimeters in a decimeter, 10 millimeters in a centimeter and 1000 microns in a millimeter?

5) There are 50 heads in a barn that has only ducks and cows. If you call the number of cows n, what do you call the number of cow legs in the barn in the math language of algebra? What do you call the number of duck legs in the barn using the math language of algebra?

Cow legs:
Duck legs:

I Can Solve Equations

When I first learned algebra, I made a terrible mistake that I have never forgotten. One of the most important rules of algebra is that you can do whatever you want to one side of an equation as long as you are fair and do the same thing to the other side of the equation. In a moment of carelessness, I forgot this rule.

You can do whatever you want to one side of the equation as long as you are fair and do it to the other side.

The equation I was working with was fairly simple: **$n - 12 = 36$**. I wanted the **n** to be all alone on one side of the equation so I added 12 to the left side of the equation. Now the **n** was all alone because -12 + 12 = 0. Unfortunately, in my hurry to solve the equation, I forgot the most important algebra rule and forgot to also add 12 to the right side of the equation. As you probably guessed, the result was horrendous. Not only did the equation get unbalanced and tip over, but the right side of the equation was so upset about the unfairness of my action that it started to cry uncontrollably.

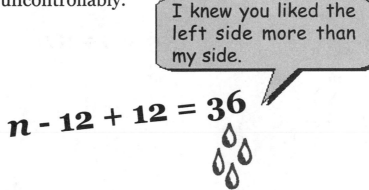

I knew you liked the left side more than my side.

$$n - 12 + 12 = 36$$

It took that equation a long time to forgive me for that mistake, but I am happy to report that for the last 20 years I have always been fair to both sides of every equation I work with. My advice to you is to please be fair to both sides of an equation. Feel free to do whatever you want to one side of an equation to help you solve it, but remember to also do exactly the same thing to the other side. I don't want another equation to go through the pain of what I did 20 years ago.

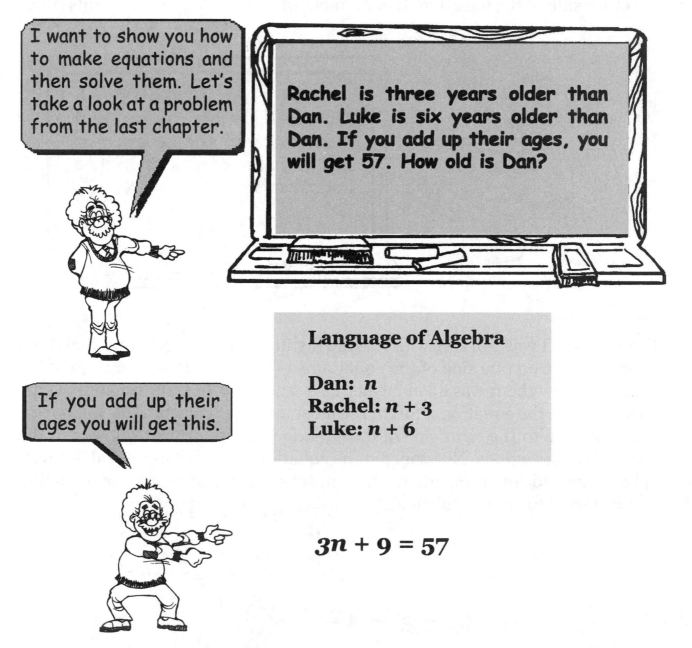

I want to show you how to make equations and then solve them. Let's take a look at a problem from the last chapter.

Rachel is three years older than Dan. Luke is six years older than Dan. If you add up their ages, you will get 57. How old is Dan?

If you add up their ages you will get this.

Language of Algebra

Dan: n
Rachel: $n + 3$
Luke: $n + 6$

$$3n + 9 = 57$$

When you are solving equations, the first thing you want to do is get the *n's* all alone on one side of the equation. In this equation, we have to get rid of the 9.

$$3n + 9 = 57$$

I know that we are allowed to subtract the 9 from that side of the equation as long as we do the exact same thing to the other side.

$$3n + 9 = 57$$
$$-9 \quad -9$$

$$3n = 48$$

Because 3 *n's* are equal to 48, we know that 1 *n* is equal to 16. Dan is 16 years old!

That was amazing! Can we do the other problem from Chapter 20?

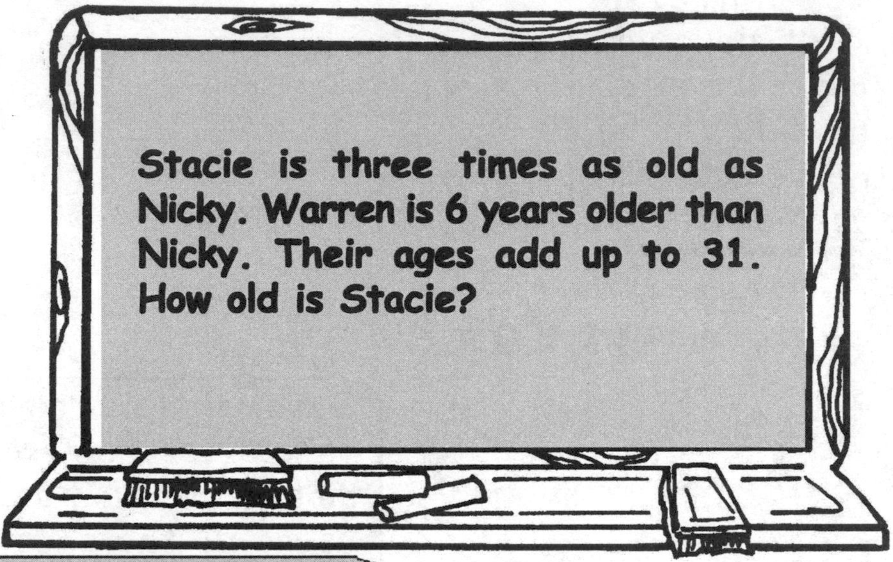

Stacie is three times as old as Nicky. Warren is 6 years older than Nicky. Their ages add up to 31. How old is Stacie?

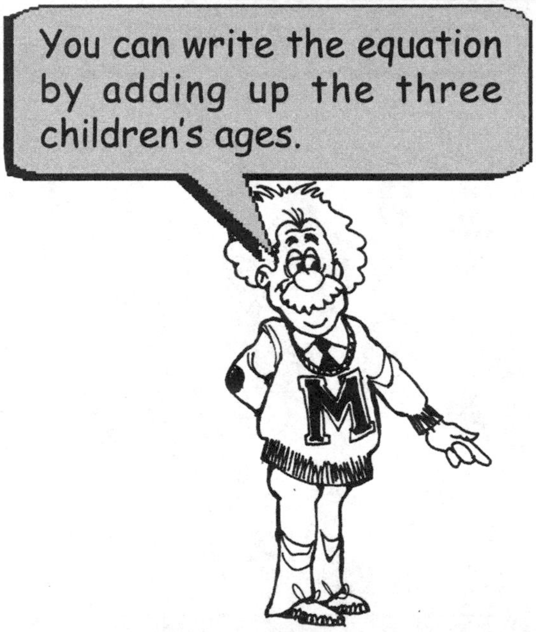

You can write the equation by adding up the three children's ages.

Language of Algebra

Nicky: n
Stacie: $3n$
Warren: $n + 6$

$$5n + 6 = 31$$

$$5n + 6 = 31$$
$$ -6 \quad -6$$

$$5n = 25$$

Now solve the equation. After you subtract 6 from both sides, you are left with **5n = 25**. Nicky is 5 years old.

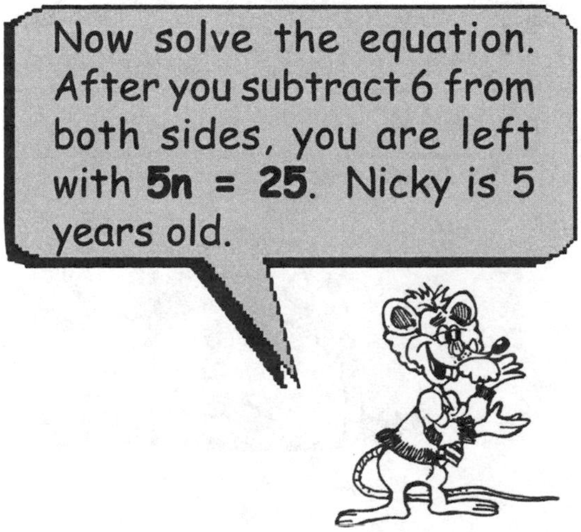

$$5n - 8 = 42$$
$$+8 \qquad +8$$

$$5n = 50$$

There are two other things you need to learn to help you solve equations. If you want to get rid of a negative 8, then you must add 8 to both sides of the equation.

That was easy! *n* must equal 10.

The other thing you need to do is collect all things that are alike. Look at this next equation. I can collect all the **n's. 5n + 3n = 8n** Now I can collect the -8 and the 10. They add up to +2.

$$5n - 8 + 3n + 10 = 42$$

$$8n + 2 = 42$$

$$8n + 2 = 42$$
$$-2 \qquad -2$$
$$8n = 40$$

$$n = 5$$

When you are solving equations, you need to follow these three steps.

Step 1: Collect things that are alike.

Step 2: Make sure the n's are alone on one side of the equation.

Step 3: Find out what one n is equal to.

I'll use the steps to solve this equation.

$$2n + 5n + 9 = 37$$

Step 1: $7n + 9 = 37$

Step 2: $7n + 9 = 37$
$$ -9 \quad -9$$
$$7n = 28$$

Step 3: $7n = 28$
$$n = 4$$

I Can Solve Equations
Level 1

1) $n + 10 = 80$

2) $2n = 100$

3) $n + 1 = 99$

4) $n + 6 = 10$

5) $n + 5 = 55$

I Can Solve Equations
Level 2

1) $n - 8 = 10$

2) $2n + 5 = 25$

3) $10n + 8 = 28$

4) $4n - 5 = 95$

5) $n - 1 = 19$

I Can Solve Equations
Level 3

1) $8n - 12 = 84$

2) $5n - 12\frac{1}{2} = 12\frac{1}{2}$

3) $100n - 11 = 89$

4) $2n + 8 + 5n + 5 = 34$

5) $11n - 9 + 9n + 9 = 100$

I Can Solve Equations
Einstein Level

1) $\frac{1}{2}n - 8 = 20$

2) $\frac{1}{4}n + 8 + \frac{1}{4}n + 5 + \frac{1}{4}n = 16$

3) $\frac{1}{8}n + 9 + \frac{7}{8}n + 9 = 20$

4) $\frac{3}{4}n - 10 + \frac{3}{4}n = 35$

5) $5 - 2n = 10$

I Can Use Algebra to Solve Problems

The principal suddenly appeared in front of Kate's math class. He looked back and forth at the surprised expressions before him. He then stepped forward and whispered a strange poem.

> I have riddles that might
> Make you shake with fright
> Because the math that you need
> To give you the speed
> To have a chance to succeed
> Is difficult indeed

He then stepped back, turned, and suddenly left the room. As he left, a small scroll fell to the floor. On the scroll were the following words.

Those classes that want an extra two hours of recess with which to play.
Must determine my age from the hints that I give you today.
Take heed though, for your time is not free.
In five minutes I'll return for your answer to see.

My age is four times my grandson's age. My son is 11 years younger than my daughter and my daughter is 30 years older than my grandson. The total of our ages is 196 years. How old am I?

The class read the hints and was instantly discouraged. They really wanted the extra recess time, but the only way they knew how to do the problem was by using guess and check. It was clear to the class that it would be impossible to solve the problem in less than five minutes.

While the class complained loudly, Kate worked furiously at her desk. Suddenly, the principal came crashing through the door. He looked around the room as he slowly spoke four words: "What is my age?" The class sat silently as the principal again asked for his age. He then turned and started to leave the room when Kate shouted from the back of the room, "You are 84 years old."

As the principal turned to face the class, a look of disbelief came over his face. He never expected anyone to solve such a difficult problem in so little time. He then placed a certificate on Kate's desk that granted the entire class an extra two hours of recess. As the principal hurried from the room, the children crowded around Kate, trying to find out how she was able to solve the problem so quickly.

You probably guessed that Kate used algebra to solve the problem. When you are using algebra to solve problems, always write down three steps.

Step 1: Turn the problem into the language of algebra

Step 2: Write an equation

Step 3: Solve the equation

Watch how I use the three steps to solve the problem that the principal gave to the children.

My age is four times my grandson's age. My son is 11 years younger than my daughter and my daughter is 30 years older than my grandson. The total of our ages is 196 years. How old am I?

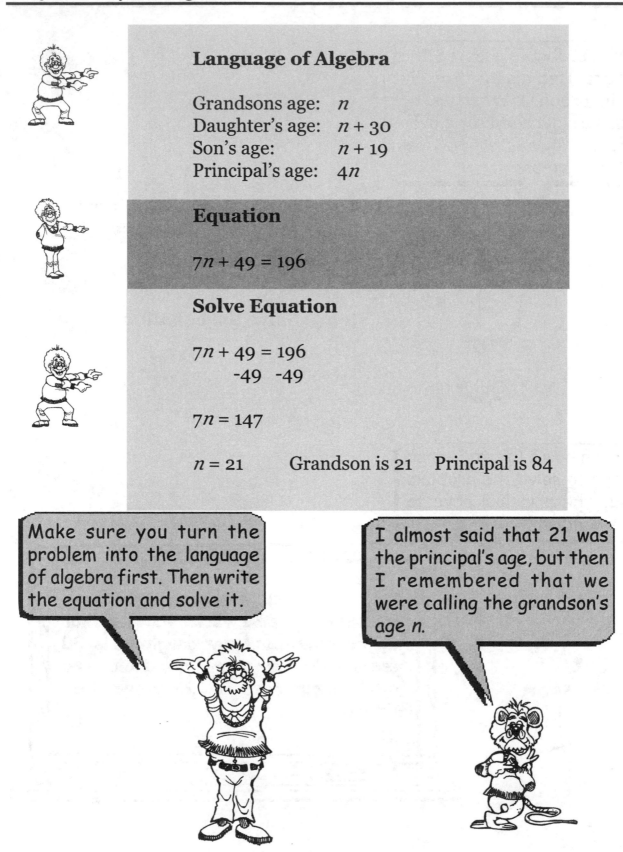

Language of Algebra

Grandsons age: n
Daughter's age: $n + 30$
Son's age: $n + 19$
Principal's age: $4n$

Equation

$7n + 49 = 196$

Solve Equation

$7n + 49 = 196$
$\quad\; -49 \quad -49$

$7n = 147$

$n = 21$ Grandson is 21   Principal is 84

Make sure you turn the problem into the language of algebra first. Then write the equation and solve it.

I almost said that 21 was the principal's age, but then I remembered that we were calling the grandson's age n.

I Can Use Algebra to Solve Problems
Level 1

1) Luke is twice as old as his brother. If you added their ages, you would get 15. How old is Luke?

Language of algebra
Luke's age:
Brother's age:

Equation:

Answer:

2) Alex weighs 5 pounds more than his dog. Altogether they weigh 105 pounds. How much does Alex weigh?

Language of algebra
Alex's weight:
Dog's weight:

Equation:

Answer:

3) A pet mouse cost $5 more than a pet snake. Adam bought a mouse and a snake and paid $25. How much did the pet mouse cost?

Language of algebra
Cost of mouse:
Cost of snake:

Equation:

Answer:

4) A giraffe at the zoo was 15 feet taller than Stanley. The heights of the giraffe and Stanley added up to 23 feet. How tall is Stanley?

Language of algebra
Stanley's height:
Giraffe's height:

Equation:

Answer:

5) Einstein weighs 120 pounds more than his pet rat. If their total weight is 130 pounds, how much does Einstein's rat weigh?

Language of algebra
Einstein's weight:
Rat's weight:

Equation:

Answer:

I Can Use Algebra to Solve Problems
Level 2

1) Anne weighs 20 pounds more than her dog. When they are on a scale together, they weigh 50 pounds. How much does Anne weigh?

Language of algebra
Dog:
Anne:

Equation:

Answer:

2) Steve's mom weighs 75 pounds more than Steve. Together they weigh 100 pounds. How much does Steve weigh?

Language of algebra
Steve:
Mom:

Equation:

Answer:

3) Ali is twice as old as his brother. If their ages add up to 60, how old is Ali?

Language of algebra
Ali's age:
Brother:

Equation:

Answer:

4) Adult movie tickets cost three times as much as children's tickets. If the cost of 1 adult ticket and 1 child's ticket is $12, what is the cost of 1 child's ticket?

Language of algebra
Adult ticket:
Child's ticket:

Equation:

Answer:

5) Dan is 35 inches taller than his baby sister. If their combined height is 89 inches, how tall is Dan's baby sister?

Language of algebra
Dan's height:
Baby's height:

Equation:

Answer:

I Can Use Algebra to Solve Problems
Level 3

1) Mary, Lindsey and Sara all have the same amount of money. If they add Rachel's $15 to their money, they will have $105. How much money does Mary have?

Language of algebra
Mary's money:
Lindsey's money:
Sara's money:
Rachel's money:

Equation:

Answer:

2) Luke, Dan and Nick all had the same amount of money. They decided to put everyone's money in a large paper sack. Unfortunately, $12 fell from the sack and was lost. Now they have $12. How much money did Luke start with?

Language of algebra
Luke's money:
Dan's money:
Nick's money:

Equation:

Answer:

3) If 8 pounds is added to 7 math books, the combined weight is 22 pounds. How much does each math book weigh?

Language of algebra
Weight of one math book:

Equation:

Answer:

4) Karen's dad gave her money for Christmas. Her mom gave her twice as much money as her dad and her little brother gave her half as much money as her dad gave her. If the total amount of money that Karen received for Christmas was $105, how much money did Karen receive from her brother?

Language of algebra
Brother's gift: n
Dad's gift:
Mom's gift:

Equation:

Answer:

5) Dave is twice as tall as Kate, who is twice as tall as Mica. Together they are 140 inches tall. How tall is Dave?

Language of algebra
Mica's height:
Kate's height:
Dave's height:

Equation:

Answer:

I Can Use Algebra to Solve Problems
Einstein Level

1) Carly is 4 years older than Stacie, who is 5 years older than Ben. If the total of their ages is 17, how old is Ben?

Language of algebra
Carly:
Stacie:
Ben:

Equation:

Answer:

2) Seth was trying to guess what page his sister was reading. She gave him the following hint: If I add the page I am reading to the page before, plus the page after, I get 276. What page is Seth's sister reading?

Language of algebra
Page sister is reading:
Page before the one she is reading:
Page after the one she is reading:

Equation:

Answer:

3) Mike thought of a number that the rest of his class was trying to guess. He told them that if you triple his number, it is the same as if you add 64 to his number. What is Mike's number?

Language of algebra
Mikes number: n

Equation:

Answer:

4) The length of a rectangle is 3 times as long as the width. If the perimeter of the rectangle is 160 feet, how wide is the rectangle?

Language of algebra
Width of rectangle:
Length of rectangle:

Equation:

Answer:

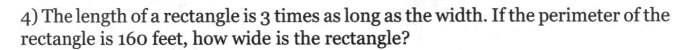

5) Jenny had twice as many dimes as nickels and 5 times as many quarters as nickels. She had the same number of pennies as she had dimes. If Jenny had 40 coins, how many quarters did she have?

Language of algebra
Number of nickels:
Number of dimes:
Number of quarters:
Numbers of pennies:

Equation:

Answer:

Radical and Squaring Machines

There is a number that you can multiply by itself and get an answer of 25. That number is obviously 5.

5 X 5 = 25

But what if I had a number like 144. Is there an easy way to find a number that can be multiplied by itself to get an answer of 144?

? x ? = 144

I have a machine called the square root machine that will easily find that number.

This square root machine is amazing. All you do is put any number in and it will tell you what number multiplied by itself equals that number. Look what happens when I put 144 into the square root machine.

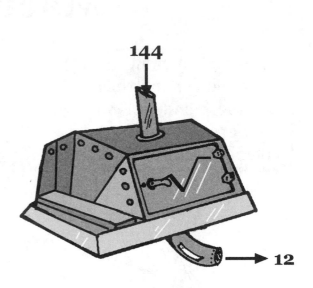

You can even put very large numbers like 1 million into the machine.

I have a secret to tell you. You really don't need my square root machine. If you can't do the problems in your head, you can use your calculator. All you do is use the $\sqrt{}$ button.

745.13
3000.10

3745.23

If you want to find the square root of 36, you would write $\sqrt{36}$.

Square roots are fun.
$\sqrt{81} = 9$
$\sqrt{64} = 8$
$\sqrt{225} = 15$

If you like square root machines, you will also like exponent machines. Exponent machines multiply numbers by themselves. Look at what happens when I put a 7 into this exponent machine.

Look at the machine. The n with the little **2** means that you multiply **7 × 7**. The machines that have n^2 on them are called squaring machines.

7

n^2

49

There are even exponent machines that multiply numbers by themselves many times. Look at this machine. The n with the little **3** means that you multiply **10 × 10 × 10**.

10

n^3

1000

Radical and Squaring Machines
Level 1

1) When you put 25 into the square root machine, what number comes out?

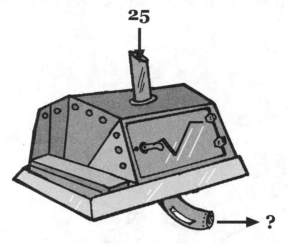

2) If you put the number 25 through a squaring machine, what number will come out?

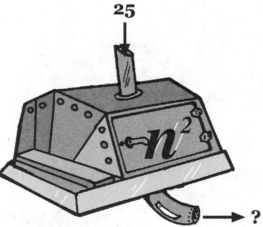

3) 6^2 =

4) If you put the number one through a squaring machine, what number will come out?

5) $\sqrt{100}$ =

Radical and Squaring Machines
Level 2

1) Ariel put a number into a square root machine. The number that came out was a 7. What number did Ariel put into the square root machine?

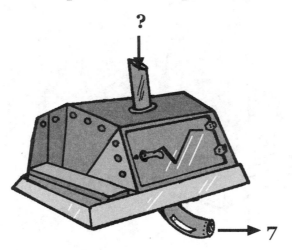

2) $\sqrt{10,000} =$

3) Is 1^5 the same as 5^1 ?

4) What number multiplied by itself equals 1,000,000?

5) Ariel put a number into a squaring machine. The number that came out was 2500. What number did Ariel put into the machine?

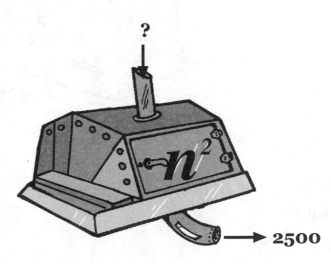

Radical and Squaring Machines
Level 3

1) Jenny put a number we'll call *n* through a squaring machine, but the number didn't change. Jenny then put the same number through a square root machine, but it still didn't change. Jenny thought that the machines were both broken, but they were working perfectly. The number Jenny used was not zero. What number did Jenny put through the machines?

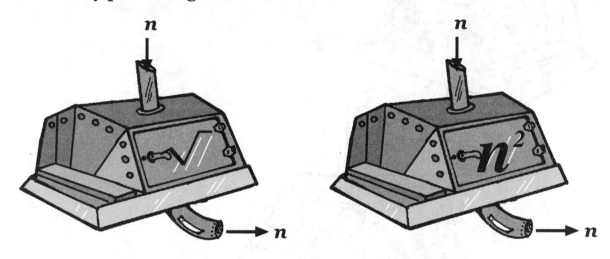

2) The volume of a cube is found by multiplying the length of the cube by its width and then by its height. The volume of the small cube shown below is 27 cubic inches because 3 x 3 x 3 = 27. If the volume of the large cube is 125 cubic inches, what is the length of each side of the cube?

3) $\sqrt{\dfrac{1}{4}} =$

4) Nate put the letter n through a squaring machine and then took the answer and put it through a square root machine. What came out of the square root machine?

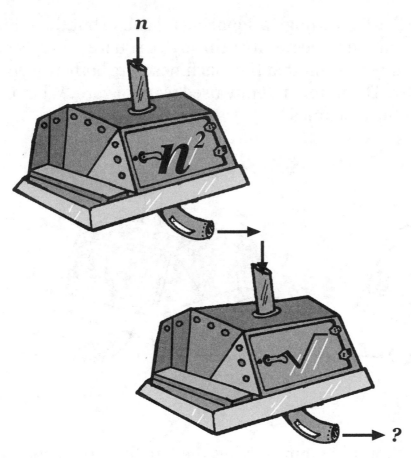

5) If you put the number 1,000,000 through a square root machine, what number would come out?

Radical and Squaring Machines
Einstein Level

1) A student put a mystery number through a square root machine. When the answer came out, she put it through another square root machine. The number 2 came out of that machine. What is the mystery number?

Mystery Number

2) What is the square root of 6.25?

3)

8 is a perfect cube because 2 x 2 x 2 = 8
27 is also a perfect cube because 3 x 3 x 3 = 27

4 is a perfect square because 2 x 2 = 4
16 is also a perfect square because 4 x 4 = 16

There is one two digit number that is both a perfect square and a perfect cube. What is that number?

4) A student put a mystery number through a squaring machine. When the answer came out, he put it through another squaring machine. The number that came out was 81. What number did he put into the first squaring machine?

Mystery Number

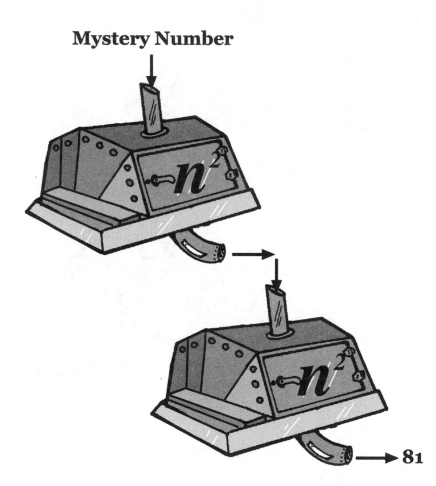

5) The area of a square dollhouse floor is 1/4 square yard. How many inches long is each side of the room?

Fantastic Formulas

Many years ago, a king and queen held a contest to find the strongest and best looking prince to marry their daughter. Unfortunately, the winner of the contest was not a very nice person.

Several years later, the time came for the youngest daughter of the king and queen to marry. This time, the king and queen decided to hold a different kind of contest. This contest would find the smartest prince in the kingdom.

The first prince sure was strong and handsome, but he wasn't very nice. I think we should look for a smart prince this time.

I agree!! The last guy was a royal pain. Let's look for somebody who is smart.

When the time came for the competition to begin, hundreds of men gathered at the castle gates. Soon the king announced that the man who answered two questions in the shortest amount of time would be allowed to ask for the hand of his daughter.

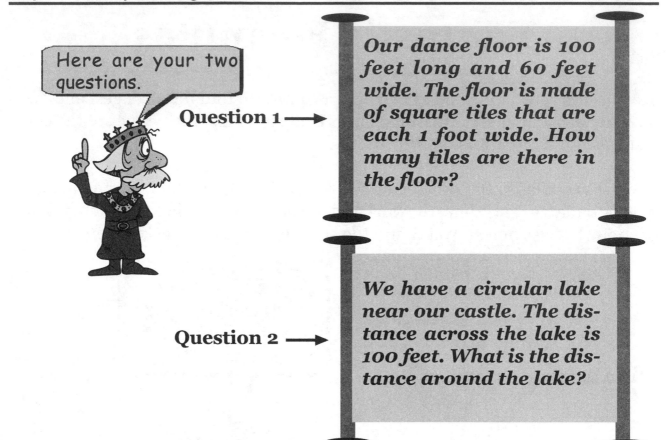

Here are your two questions.

Question 1 →

Our dance floor is 100 feet long and 60 feet wide. The floor is made of square tiles that are each 1 foot wide. How many tiles are there in the floor?

Question 2 →

We have a circular lake near our castle. The distance across the lake is 100 feet. What is the distance around the lake?

Hundreds of men ran into the castle and started counting the floor tiles. One prince stayed behind and slowly walked up to the king and queen.

There are 6000 tiles in your dance floor and the distance around the lake is 314 feet.

After the prince gave his answer, the king and queen declared that the contest was over. A few weeks later, the prince married the king and queen's daughter and became the highly paid chief of mathematics for the kingdom.

How did the prince know the answers to the questions without measuring or counting?

The prince found the answers by using formulas. To find how many tiles were in the floor, the prince simply multiplied the length of the floor by the width.

If a floor was 5 feet wide and 10 feet long, it would have 5 rows with 10 tiles in each row.

Row 1 →
Row 2 →
Row 3 →
Row 4 →
Row 5 →

Each tile is 1 square foot, so the area would be 50 square feet.

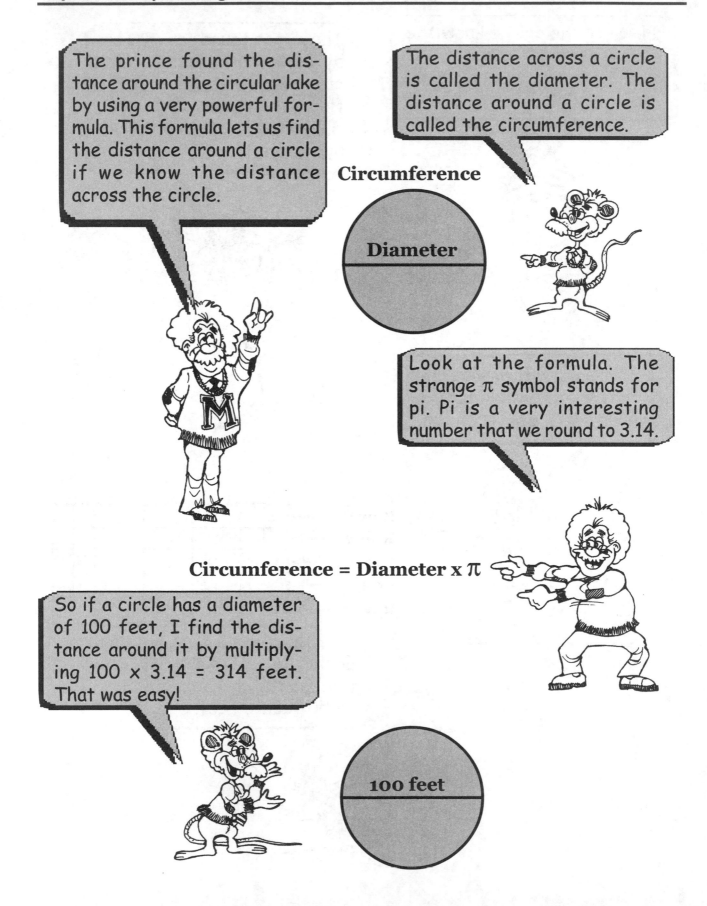

The prince found the distance around the circular lake by using a very powerful formula. This formula lets us find the distance around a circle if we know the distance across the circle.

The distance across a circle is called the diameter. The distance around a circle is called the circumference.

Circumference

Diameter

Look at the formula. The strange π symbol stands for pi. Pi is a very interesting number that we round to 3.14.

Circumference = Diameter x π

So if a circle has a diameter of 100 feet, I find the distance around it by multiplying 100 x 3.14 = 314 feet. That was easy!

100 feet

Fantastic Formulas
Level 1

1) King Arthur had 9 knights around his round table. If each knight took up 4 feet of space and King Arthur took up 5 feet, what was the circumference of the round table?

2) A redwood tree has a trunk that is 15 feet thick. What is the distance around the trunk?

3) If the diameter of a coin is one inch, what is the circumference of that coin?

4) If the Earth is 8000 miles in diameter, what is the distance around the Earth?

5) If the moon is 2000 miles in diameter, what is the distance around the moon?

Fantastic Formulas
Level 2

1) Tiles that are 1 square foot are selling for $2 each. What would be the cost of tiles for a room that is 20 feet long and 10 feet wide?

2) How many square feet are in a square yard?

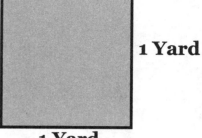

1 Yard

1 Yard

3) If Bernardo runs 1 foot each second, how many seconds will it take him to run around a circular lake that has a diameter of 1000 feet?

4) If 1 foot by 1 foot tiles weigh 3 pounds each, what is the weight of the tiles that cover a floor that is 5 feet wide and 10 feet long?

5) If the diameter of a circle is 1 foot, what is its circumference?

a) 3 feet
b) 4 feet
c) Pi feet (π)

Fantastic Formulas
Level 3

1) How many square inches are in a square yard?

2) The Earth has a diameter that is 4 times the diameter of the Moon. Does this mean that the Earth's circumference is 4 times larger than the Moon's circumference?

3) How many tiles that are 3 feet by 3 feet will it take to cover a floor that is 9 feet wide and 90 feet long?

90 feet

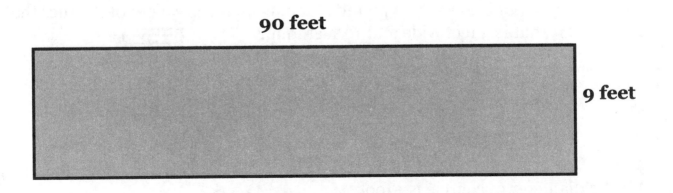

9 feet

4) Maria wants to build the first tire that has a circumference of 1 mile. How many feet tall will the tire be? (Round to the nearest foot.)

Did you know that there are 5280 feet in each mile?

5) How many 1 foot by 1 foot tiles will it take to cover the floor shown below?

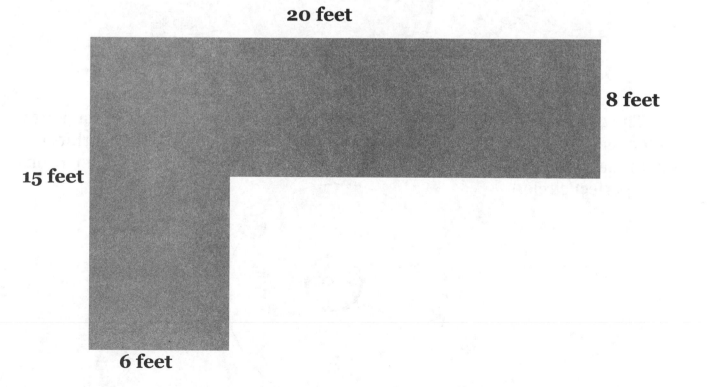

20 feet

8 feet

15 feet

6 feet

Fantastic Formulas
Einstein Level

1) King Arthur wanted a circular table built that was large enough for 16 people. If each person had 4 feet of space, what should the diameter of the table be? (Round to the nearest foot.)

2) Ben can go to school by walking around a circular lake or by canoeing across it. If the lake is 2 miles across, how much longer is his trip if he decides to walk around the lake instead of canoeing across it?

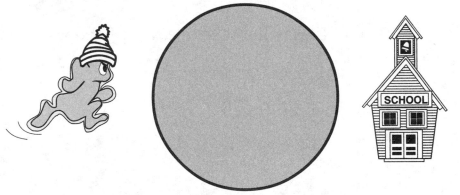

3) The center of the Moon is about 250,000 miles from the center of the Earth. What is the distance it travels during 1 orbit of the Earth? (The Moon orbits in a path that is not a perfect circle, but for this problem we will pretend that it orbits in a perfect circle.)

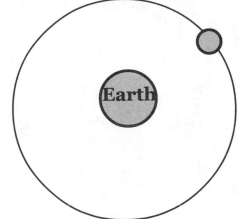

4) If you divide the circumference of any circle by its diameter, you will get the same answer. What is the answer?

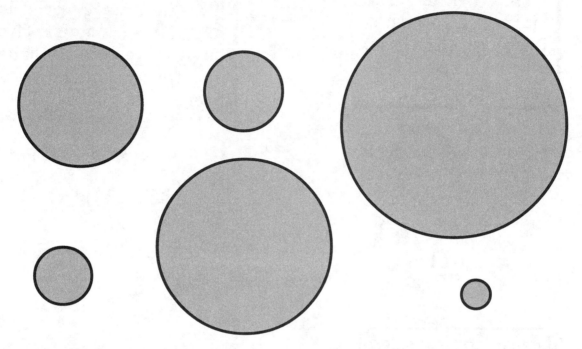

5) Carpet sells for $27 a square yard at a furniture store. The store thinks the price sounds too expensive, so it is going to start selling carpet by the square foot. What should they charge for each square foot if they want to keep the price the same as $27 a square yard?

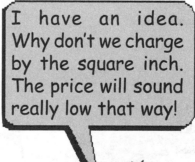

I have an idea. Why don't we charge by the square inch. The price will sound really low that way!

I Can Answer That Question

Here's another thinking question. Is the statement on the blackboard true?

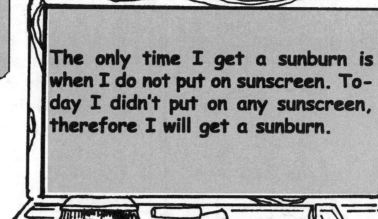

The only time I get a sunburn is when I do not put on sunscreen. Today I didn't put on any sunscreen, therefore I will get a sunburn.

My first thought is that it is true, but then I thought of many ways it would not be true.

1) If I don't wear sunscreen and I stay indoors all day, I won't get a sunburn.

2) If I don't wear sunscreen and it rains all day, I won't get a sunburn.

3) If I don't wear sunscreen and I wear heavy clothes, I will not get a sunburn.

That was a tricky question. I really have to be careful with my thinking. My head really hurts. I wonder if it is from thinking too hard?

Here is an interesting thinking problem:

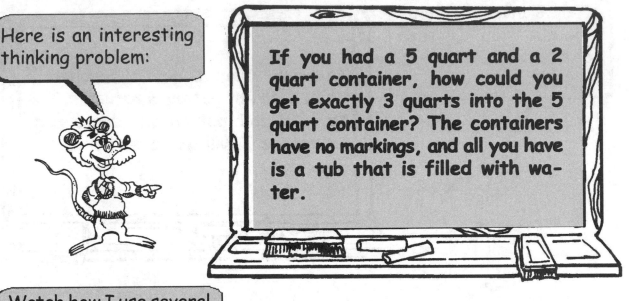

If you had a 5 quart and a 2 quart container, how could you get exactly 3 quarts into the 5 quart container? The containers have no markings, and all you have is a tub that is filled with water.

Watch how I use several steps to solve this problem.

Sorry Einstein, that was way over my head!!

Step 1: Fill the 2 quart container and pour it into the 5 quart container.

Step 2: Fill the 2 quart container again and pour it into the 5 quart container. You now have 4 quarts in the 5 quart container.

Step 3: Fill the 2 quart container again and pour as much as you can into the 5 quart container. Now you have 1 quart left in the 2 quart container.

Step 4: Empty the 5 quart container and pour the 1 quart from the 2 quart container into the empty 5 quart.

Step 5: Fill the 2 quart container again and pour it into the 5 quart container. Now you have 3 quarts in the 5 quart container.

I Can Answer That Question
Level 1

1) Paul never skateboards without his helmet. Paul is skateboarding. Do we know he is wearing his helmet?

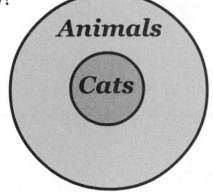

2) We know that all squares are rectangles. Does that mean that all rectangles must be squares?

We are all squares, but we are also rectangles!

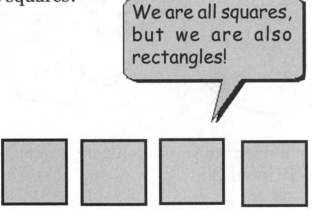

3) Which drawing best shows that all cats are animals, but not all animals are cats? Why?

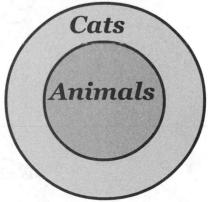

4) A school decided to make coins that could be used to buy lunches at the school. The value of a mosquito coin is the same as a mouse coin. The value of a mouse coin is the same as a moose coin. Does this mean that the value of a mosquito coin is the same as a moose coin?

5) If we know that all left-handed children are very intelligent and Nate is left-handed, do we know that Nate is very intelligent?

I Can Answer That Question
Level 2

1) Luke is older than Rachel and Daniel is younger than Rachel. Who is older, Luke or Daniel?

2) If Alice does not clean her room, she will not get her allowance. If Alice didn't get her allowance, do we know that she didn't clean her room? Why ?

3) If an angle is less than 90°, it is called an acute angle. Angle A is not an acute angle. What do we know about angle A?

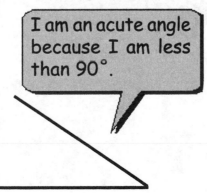

I am an acute angle because I am less than 90°.

4) If it is raining, I will be cold if I am outdoors. It is raining and I am outdoors. Do you know that I am cold?

5) Paul never plays ice hockey without his helmet. Paul is wearing his helmet. Do we know that he is playing ice hockey?

I Can Answer That Question
Level 3

1) If it is raining, I will get wet if I go outside. I went outside and got wet. Do you know it was raining when I went outside?

2) If you dress in a suit, you will be popular. If Ted is popular, do we know that he dresses in a suit?

3) Mavis is twice as old as Claire. Steve is one year older than Claire. Can you tell who the oldest child is?

4) You have two containers. One holds exactly 3 quarts. The other holds exactly 5 quarts. There are **no** markings on the containers that allow you to know when they contain one, two, or four quarts.

You have a tub full of water and you can fill and empty the 3 and 5 quart containers however you wish. How can you end up with exactly 4 quarts in the 5 quart container?

5) All the teachers at Einstein Elementary School who picked blue as their favorite color are left-handed. Ed is a teacher at Einstein Elementary School and is left-handed. Do we know that Ed's favorite color is blue?

I Can Answer That Question
Einstein Level

1) If Stanley drinks coffee before he goes to bed, he will get very little sleep. If he gets very little sleep, he will fail the big test. If he fails the big test, he won't get into his favorite college. From this information, can we say that if Stanley drinks coffee before he goes to bed, he will not get into his favorite college?

2) You have two containers. One holds exactly 7 quarts. The other holds exactly 9 quarts. There are **no** markings on the containers that allow you to know when they contain one, two, three, four, five, six or eight quarts.

You have a tub full of water and you can fill and empty the 7 and 9 quart containers however you wish. How can you end up with exactly 8 quarts in the 9 quart container?

3) Car accidents occur more often within 30 miles of one's home. Because of this, it is safer to drive when you are at least 30 miles away from your home. Is this statement true? Why or why not?

4) Phil is going on a 12 mile bike trip. In addition to the two tires on his bike, Phil also has a spare tire. If he wants all three tires to go the same distance, how many miles will each tire go during his 12 mile trip? (Hint: The answer is not 4 miles because you do not ride a bike on one tire.)

5) A rat stood on the middle rung of a ladder. It went up 8 rungs and then down 10. It then went up 5 and then down 16. It is now standing on the bottom rung. How many rungs does this ladder have?

Why do we Need Decimals?

If you wanted .238 of the worm, then cut it into 1000 equal pieces and take 238 of them.

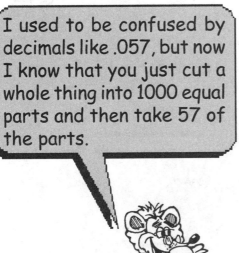

I used to be confused by decimals like .057, but now I know that you just cut a whole thing into 1000 equal parts and then take 57 of the parts.

Thousandths

Whole

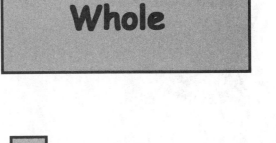

← .057 of the whole

Why do we Need Decimals?
Level 1

1) Paul wanted .6 of a candy bar. He cut the candy bar into 10 equal pieces and then took _____ of them.

I'm glad you are finally sending other things through the machine.

2) If Joy was allowed to spend .45 of her savings, what machine should she put her money through?

a) Tenths
b) Hundredths
c) Thousandths

3) A group of children were going to each receive .22 of a pile of money. Explain how they could find .22 of the money by using machines.

4) Janelle had .4 of a pie and Joe had .3 of a pie. If they combined their pieces, how much of the pie would they have?

5) Dan had a whole pie on Thursday. If he ate .2 of the pie on Friday, how much would be remaining?

Why do we Need Decimals?
Level 2

1) Which decimal is larger, **.4** or **.05**?

2) Stephanie had $1. She decided to find out how much money .47 of her dollar was. Stephanie was about to put the dollar through the hundredths machine when she realized that she already knew the answer. Why did Stephanie know the answer before she put the money through the machine?

3) Kate needed to find .1 of a worm. She planned to put the worm through the tenths machine and then take 1 piece. Unfortunately, she put the worm through the hundredths machine by mistake. How many of the pieces that came out of the hundredths machine should she take?

4) If Kate wants .1 of a worm, but put it through the thousandths machine instead of the tenths machine, how many of the pieces that came out of the thousandths machine should she take?

5) If you put a $1 bill through the tenths machine, what coin would come out?

Why do we Need Decimals?
Level 3

1) The decimal .53 is equal to $\frac{5}{10} + \frac{3}{100}$.   The decimal .42 is equal to $\frac{?}{10} + \frac{?}{100}$.

2) Which decimal is larger, .09 or .1?

3) If you put \$10,000 through a thousandths machine, how much money is each part equal to?

4) The decimal .345 is equal to $\frac{3}{10} + \frac{4}{100} + \frac{5}{1000}$.

The decimal .798 is equal to $\frac{?}{10} + \frac{?}{100} + \frac{?}{1000}$.

5) Ethan started with 1 pie. If he ate .28 of the pie, how much is remaining?

Why do we Need Decimals?
Einstein Level

1) Which decimal is larger, .099999 or .100001?

2) If you sent a 50 ton whale through the thousandths machine, how much would each piece weigh?

3) If you wanted to find .3274 of something, you would need to find a machine that would cut things into _____ pieces.

4) The decimal .8492 is equal to $\dfrac{?}{10} + \dfrac{?}{100} + \dfrac{?}{1000} + \dfrac{?}{10,000}$

5) Lou started with a whole candy bar and ate .3875 of it. Write a decimal for the amount that Lou has left.

I Cannot Understand a Thing You are Saying

There once were three amoebas who lived on three different islands. They all spoke the same language so they could talk to each other. The only time they had a problem was when they started talking about parts of things. If they talked about an apple being half eaten, the first amoeba said it was 50% gone while the second amoeba said it was .5 gone. The third amoeba, who only used fractions, said it was 1/2 gone.

The arguing went on and on because the amoebas didn't understand that they were saying the same thing, but only in a different way.

Percents, decimals and fractions are all used to talk about parts of things. You can use my translation chart to help you understand what your fellow amoebas are talking about.

I think this chart is going to help me.

Percents	Fractions	Decimals
50%	1/2	.5
15%	3/20	.15
80%	8/10	.8
1%	1/100	.01
53%	53/100	.53
100%	1/1	1
600%	6/1	6

I Cannot Understand a Thing you are Saying
Level 1

1) Translate what the amoeba is saying into the language of the others.

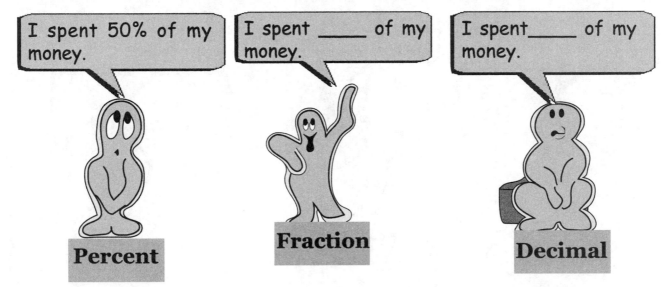

2) Change 25% into the fraction language and the decimal language.

3) Change .75 into the fraction and percent language.

4) Translate what the amoeba is saying into the language of the others.

5) What is .1 as a percent? What is .1 as a fraction?

I Cannot Understand a Thing you are Saying
Level 2

1) Translate the fraction into the percent and decimal language.

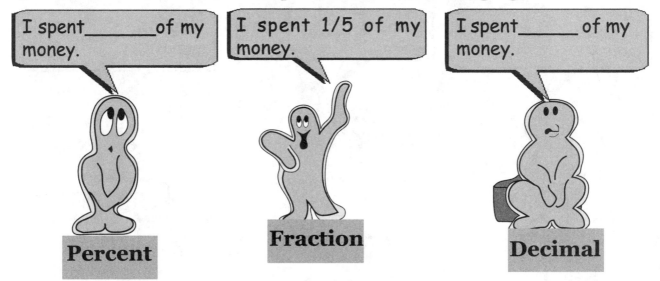

2) Many fractions are equal to 1. 2/2 and 5/5 are both ways of saying 1. How would the amoeba who only speaks percents say 1?

3) Write 5% as a decimal and a fraction.

4) Translate the decimal into the percent and fraction language.

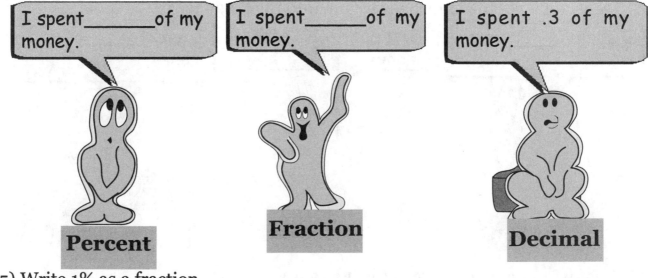

5) Write 1% as a fraction.

I Cannot Understand a Thing you are Saying Level 3

1) Write 200% as a fraction.

2) Translate the fraction into the language of percents and the decimal language.

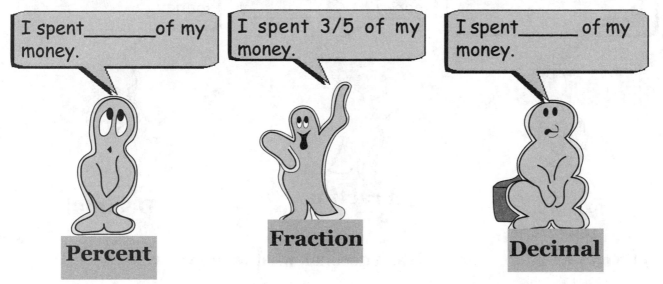

3) Write .02 as a fraction.

4) Translate the percent into the fraction and decimal language.

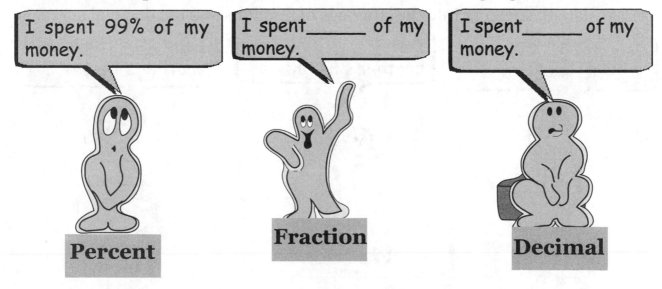

5) How would the decimal-speaking amoeba say 500%?

I Cannot Understand a Thing you are Saying
Einstein Level

1) Translate the percent into the language of fractions and the decimal language.

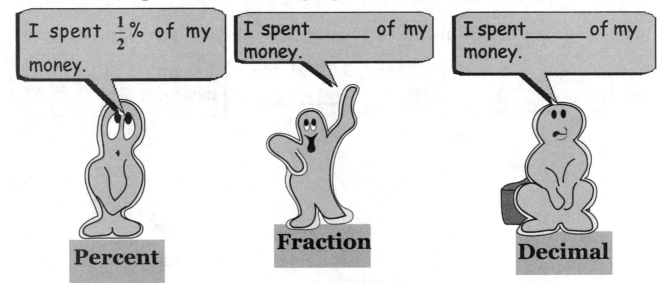

2) If you wanted to write 101% as a decimal, what would you write?

3) Write $33\frac{1}{3}$% as a fraction and as a decimal.

4) Translate the percent into the language of fractions and the decimal language.

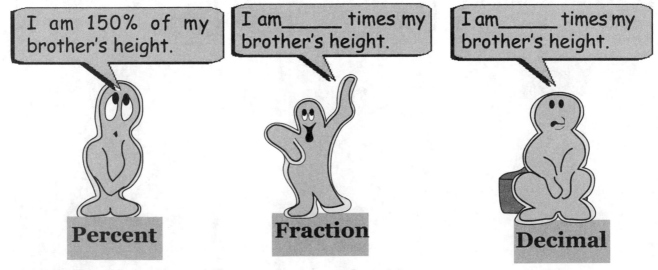

5) Is there any difference between .5% and 50%?

Chapter 1

Level 1
1) 32, 34, 36
2) $2
3) $50
4) 50
5) 25

Level 2
1) 20, 24, 28
2) $8
3) 29
4) 100,000
5) December 6th

Level 3
1) Sunday
2) -15
3) 80
4) 125
5) $12.50

Einstein
1) 25 pounds   The numbers are perfect squares.

2) 1/9   Divide by 3

3) 1/16 pie left   Divide 1/8 of the pie in half.

4) 1/32   Divide by 2

5) 7:00   1:00 is 2 pounds; 2:00 is 4 pounds; 3:00 is 8 pounds and so forth.

Chapter 2

Level 1
1) No
2) 5 egg carrying ants
3) 10 children
4) Yes
5) 6 rats

Level 2
1) 3 people
2) 1000 cans
3) 10 cans
4) 16 acorns
5) 20 children

Level 3
1) 60 papers
2) Yes
3) 16 people
4) 16,017
5) No

Einstein

1) 100 people   15,000 pound limit allows one hundred 150 pound people

2) Yes   4000 ounces is equal to 250 pounds.

3) 16 inches   5 quarters per ounce equals 240 quarters for 3 pounds. 240 quarters are 16" tall because it takes 15 quarters to make one inch in height.

4) 640 pints   80 gallons weigh 720 pounds. There are 640 pints in 80 gallons.

5) 98 bags   4905 pounds of weight available for sand. 4905 divided by 50 pounds is 98.1 bags.

Chapter 3

Level 1
1) 5 for $24
2) $18
3) 10¢
4) $8
5) $3

Level 2
1) 25¢
2) $1.00
3) $10.50
4) 4 for 60¢
5) $18.20

Level 3
1) Saturday
2) 40¢
3) $3.20
4) $8
5) Store B

Einstein
1) 50¢ — A very common wrong answer is $1.00. If the candy bar was $1.00, then the hot dog would be $4 more or $5.

2) $75 — They will need 50 gallons of gas.

3) 16¢ — There are 16 cups in a gallon. 16¢ times 16 equals $2.56.

4) $111.60 — There are 31 days in December times 24 hours equals 744 hours. 744 times 15¢ equals $111.60.

5) $10 — A centimeter is 1/100 of a meter. 1/100 of $1000 is $10.

Chapter 4

Level 1
1) $20
2) Three pennies
3) 90¢
4) 3¢
5) 25 dimes

Level 2
1) $7.50
2) $1.15
3) 12¢
4) 25¢
5) $6.60

Level 3
1) $1.55
2) $10.03
3) So the change would come out even.
4) $87.05
5) $9.00

Einstein
1) 10¢   Each ball is 1¢ less than $10. So 10 balls are 10¢ less than $100.

2) $1.00 $50 + $25 + $10 + $5 + $1 = $91 $92 - $91 = $1.00

3) $7.50   Each Canadian dollar in price is only 75 cents in United States money. $10 in Canadian money therefore is worth $7.50 in United States money.

4) $89.04   Cost is almost $1000 + $100 + $10 + $1 or $1111   Change would be $89 plus 4¢.

5) $12.50

Chapter 5

Level 1
1) 1/2 pound
2) 1/4 pie
3) 8 ounces
4) 1 pound
5) 1500 pounds

Level 2
1) 8 ounces
2) 1/8 pie
3) 3/4 pounds
4) 1/4 pound
5) 500 pounds

Level 3

1) $2\frac{1}{4}$ pounds

2) 1500 pounds
3) 1/8 pound
4) 7/16 of a pie
5) 1/2 way because he weighs twice as much as the child

Einstein
1) 14 ounces

2) $1\frac{7}{8}$ pounds

3) 4 ounces $\frac{1}{4}$ pound equals 4 ounces

4) 1 pound   1/2000 of a ton is equal to one pound

5) 23 pints

Chapter 6

Level 1
1) 15 eggs
2) 27 apples
3) 10 people
4) 2 cups of oats

5) $1\frac{1}{2}$ cups of sugar

Level 2

1) $1\frac{1}{4}$ cups of flour

2) 5 apples
3) 2 days
4) 1/4 teaspoon
5)   3 cups of milk
        6 cups of oats

        $3\frac{3}{4}$ cups of flour

        6 cups of raisins

Level 3
1) 4 cups of raisins
2) 10 eggs
3) 10 people

4) $7\frac{1}{2}$ days

5) 1/8 teaspoon

Einstein

1) $2\frac{1}{4}$ pounds   Each 25 cookies uses 3/4 of a pound of bananas.

2) 9 days   The box will last one person for 36 days. It will last 4 people 9 days.

3) 5 people $2\frac{1}{2}$ gallons is 1/4 of 10 gallons. 5 people are 1/4 of 20 people.

4) $1\frac{1}{4}$ eggs   5 pancakes are 1/8 of 40. $1\frac{1}{4}$ is 1/8 of 10 eggs.

5) Sugar: $1\frac{1}{4}$ cups   Oats: $2\frac{1}{2}$ cups

Chapter 7

Level 1
1) $730
2) 144 donuts
3) $7.08
4) 1700 pounds
5) 160 ounces

Level 2
1) 196 hoses
2) 3750 feet
3) 3600 inches
4) $506.25
5) $98

Level 3
1) 289 days
2) 29,400 feet
3) 5280 feet
4) 86,400 seconds
5) $48.65

Einstein
1) $6297.60
2) 1,000,000 microns
3) 16,070,400,000 miles
4) $207.36
5) 64 cups

Chapter 8

Level 1
1) 24 legs
2) 110 legs
3) 38 legs
4) 100 fingers
5) 300 legs

Level 2
1) 8 spiders
2) Same amount of legs
3) 31 legs
4) 179 legs
5) 808 legs

Level 3
1) 1680 legs
2) 256 legs
3) 32 duck legs
4) May 9th
5) 80 shoes which is 40 pairs of shoes

Einstein
1) 7020 legs   30 total cats (120 legs); 150 fleas (900 legs); 750 spiders (6000 legs)

2) 100,000,000 legs   10,000 boxes; 1,000,000 centipedes;   100,000,000 legs

3) 10 ducks   Guess and check

4) 6060 legs   12 legs for farmers;   36 barrels; 216 cats (864) legs);
1296 kittens (5184 legs)

5) 20,736 pennies   144 chickens x 12 = 1728 eggs x 12 = 20,736 pennies

Chapter 9

Level 1
1) 5 pounds
2) 250 pounds
3) 1 foot
4) $750
5) $35

Level 2
1) $3
2) $8642.31
3) 3/4
4) 1¢
5) 100%

Level 3
1) $80
2) $63.75
3) 19/20
4) $65
5) $13.50   10% = $9   5% = $4.50   15% = $9 + $4.50 = $13.50

Einstein

1) 50¢   1% is $1.00 $\frac{1}{2}$% is 50¢

2) 300%

3) $110.77   45% off is $85.50   New price is $104.50   Tax is .06 x $104.50 = $6.27

4) $21   100% is $12   75% is $9 $12 + $9 = $21

5) $2.20   1% = $8.80 $\frac{1}{4}$% = $2.20

Chapter 10

Level 1
1) 70 flies
2) $25
3) 30 chickens
4) 3 cups
5) 10 days

Level 2
1) One pound
2) 15 minutes
3) 15 days
4) 500 steps
5) $0

Level 3

1) $10\frac{1}{2}$ cups

2) 1 hour

3) $2\frac{1}{2}$ carrots

4) 5 hours
5) 6 pounds

Einstein

1) $47\frac{1}{2}$ One ounce will last 5 days. 9.5 times 5 equals $47\frac{1}{2}$

2) 15 quarts   12 quarts for 8 miles means $1\frac{1}{2}$ for each mile.

3) 1 minute   60 miles in 60 minutes is one mile each minute.

4) 100 hours   Snail will crawl 10 meters in 60 minutes, or an hour. To crawl 1000 meters would be 100 times one hour or 100 hours.

5) One hour   Dave paints 1/4 of the car in an hour. Kate paints 1/4 of the car in an hour. Melissa paints 1/2 of the car in an hour. The three fractions add up to one whole car.

Chapter 11

Level 1
1) 200 feet
2) 50 feet
3) 200 feet
4) 20 inches

5) $6\frac{1}{2}$ inches

Level 2
1) 14 inches
2) 40 feet
3) 30 feet
4) 95 feet
5) 5 feet

Level 3
1) 25 feet
2) 80 feet
3) 50 feet
4) 20 feet
5) 18 inches

Einstein

1) 4 inches   The yardstick is three times the height of the shadow. One foot is three times as long as 4 inches.

2) 60 feet   The stick's shadow is $1\frac{1}{2}$ the length of the tree. A 90 foot long shadow is $1\frac{1}{2}$ times 60 feet.

3) 5 feet   The house is 6 times the shadow. 60 inches (or 5 feet) is 6 times 10 inches.

4) 25 feet   The giant's shadow was 5 times Jack's shadow, so the giant must be 5 times Jack's height.

5) $1\frac{1}{2}$ inches   The rat's shadow is 1/24 of the actual size of the rat. 1/24 of 36 inches is $1\frac{1}{2}$ inches.

Chapter 12

Level 1
1) 10 times
2) 500 times
3) 400 red marbles
4) 3 miles
5) 6 children

Level 2
1) 30 apples
2) 40 minutes
3) 1/2 mile
4) 25 times
5) $520

Level 3
1) 3 hours
2) 50 red jelly beans
3) $1\frac{1}{2}$ miles
4) 3 boxes
5) 16 seconds

Einstein
1) 6 feet — Brianna's shadow is 3/4 of her height. 3/4 of 6 feet is equal to 4 feet 6 inches.

2) 75 times — The A space is 1/16 of the circle. 1/16 of 1200 is 75.

3) 72 students — Spring is 1/4 of the year. 1/4 of 288 is 72.

4) 2 miles — The distance to the mountain and back is 4 miles. Therefore it is 2 miles to the mountain.

5) Count the time it takes sound to reach your ears after the lightning. Because sound takes 5 seconds to travel one mile, divide this time by five.

Chapter 13

Level 1
1) -$1
2) $0
3) 5 degrees
4) -$5
5) -$20

Level 2
1) -$10
2) -5
3) -5°F
4) -$20
5) 13 miles

Level 3
1) $9
2) 20 degrees
3) 50 cents
4) -$8
5) 220 degrees

Einstein
1) $6   Samantha had $8, but she owed her grandmother $17, so she really has -$9. Her grandmother gave her $5 so Samantha now has -$4. When the grandmother takes away $10 of debt, it is just like giving her $10. -$4 + $10 = $6

2) 2 days   The second day the snake starts at the one foot mark and climbs 5 feet to the top of the well. It is therefore out of the well on the second day.

3) 671.6 degrees

4) 10:00 P.M.   The good clock went 12 hours. The broken clock goes 50 minutes each hour. 12 x 50 = 600 minutes or 10 hours.

5) 43 degrees   The difference between 10° and -33° is 43 degrees.

Chapter 14

Level 1
1) $1.50
2) 5:30
3) $20
4) 10¢
5) $25

Level 2
1) 8 ounces
2) $7.25

3) $2\frac{1}{2}$ miles

4) 20 jelly beans
5) 5:30

Level 3
1) 4 cups
2) 90 seconds
3) $8.30

4) $2\frac{1}{4}$ inches

5) 25¢

Einstein
1) One hour and 40 minutes

Five hours is 300 minutes. They each should work 100 minutes.

2) 512 days

128 ounces in a gallon. The medicine lasts 4 days for `each ounce.

3) 1/12 pound

If you split 1/4 into 3 pieces, you would get 1/12.

4) 6:20

5) $80

Sammy gave away 15/16 of his money. Sammy has 1/16 left and that is equal to $5. If 1/16 is equal to $5, then 16/16 is equal to $80.

Chapter 15

Level 1
1) 10 miles
2) 2.5 miles
3) 80 miles
4) 2 miles
5) 15 feet

Level 2
1) 6 miles each hour
2) 6 hours

3) $2\frac{1}{2}$ seconds

4) 2 miles
5) 1 mile

Level 3
1) 20 miles
2) 140 miles
3) 5 miles
4) 8:00 A.M.
5) 11,160,000 miles

Einstein

1) 1 mile

60 miles per hour is 60 miles per 60 minutes, which is 1 mile per minute.

2) $2\frac{1}{2}$ miles

Sound takes 5 seconds to go one mile, so it would go 2.5 miles in 12.5 seconds.

3) 10 miles per hour

If you run one mile in 6 minutes, then you run 10 miles in one hour because 60 minutes is 6 x 10.

4) 5 miles per hour

12 minutes=one mile   24 minutes=2 miles
36 minutes=3 miles   48 minutes=4 miles
60 minutes=5 miles

5) $5\frac{1}{2}$ miles

$27\frac{1}{2}$ seconds $\div 5 = 5\frac{1}{2}$

Chapter 16

Level 1
1) 5 hours
2) 1/2 hour
3) 4 hours
4) 5:00
5) 20 hours

Level 2
1) 10 hours
2) 4 hours
3) 5 hours
4) 8 hours
5) 6 hours

Level 3
1) 30 minutes
2) 6:00 P.M.
3) 80 hours
4) $2\frac{1}{2}$ hours
5) $3\frac{1}{2}$ hours

Einstein
1) 20 hours   5 miles divided by 1/4 hour is equal to 20 hours.

2) 12:12 P.M.   5 miles in an hour means 1 mile in 1/5 of an hour or 12 minutes.

3) $2\frac{1}{2}$ hours   1/10 fits into 1/4 two and a half times.

4) 15 minutes   The cheetah goes 70 miles in one hour; 35 miles in 1/2 hour, so it would go 17.5 miles (half of 35) in 15 minutes.

5) 12 minutes   160 miles is 1/5 of 800 miles, so it would take the jet 1/5 of an hour or 12 minutes.

Chapter 17

Level 1
1) 5 miles per hour
2) 30 miles per hour
3) 2.5 miles per hour
4) 6 miles per hour
5) 14 miles per hour

Level 2
1) 120 miles per hour
2) 12 miles per hour
3) 25 miles per hour
4) 30 miles per hour
5) 200 miles per hour

Level 3
1) 1/5 mile per hour
2) 1 mile per hour
3) 4000 miles per hour
4) 10 miles per hour
5) 8 miles per hour

Einstein

1) 720 miles per hour — Find how many seconds there are in one hour? (60 x 60 = 3600) How many 5 second parts are in 3600? (3600÷5=720)

2) 669,600,000 — 3600 seconds in an hour x 186,000 miles each second.

3) 60 miles per hour — One mile per minute is 60 miles in 60 minutes.

4) 18,000 miles per hour — $27,000 \div 1\frac{1}{2} = 18,000$

5) $7\frac{1}{2}$ miles per hour — 8 minutes for one mile. How many 8 minute parts are in one hour?

There are $7\frac{1}{2}$.

Chapter 18

Level 1
1) 4000 pounds
2) 1/2 pound
3) $2\frac{1}{2}$ tons
4) 30 pounds
5) 1/4 pound

Level 2
1) 625 pounds
2) $7\frac{1}{2}$ pounds
3) 1/4 pound
4) 2 pounds
5) 40 pounds

Level 3
1) 36 pounds
2) 6 ounces
3) No
4) 850 pounds   (15% is 150 pounds)
5) 56 pounds

Einstein

1) 3/4 pound   16 cups in a gallon. 24 pounds ÷ 16 = $1\frac{1}{2}$ pounds per cup.

This means 3/4 pound per 1/2 cup.

2) 144 ounces or 9 pounds   There are 12 x 12 = 144 one by one pieces in the one foot square.

3) 2 ounces   16 pounds equals 16 x 16 = 256 ounces of weight.
128 fluid ounces in a gallon, so 1 fluid ounce is equal to 2 ounces of weight.

4) 1 ounce for an inch   A meter weighs 39 ounces. There are 39 inches in a meter, so 1 inch equals 1 ounce.

5) 1 ounce   12 donuts=48 ounces; 1 donut = 4 ounces; 1/4 donut = 1 ounce

Chapter 19

Level 1
1) 110 pounds
2) 10 hours
3) 394 inches
4) 2 yards
5) Mile

Level 2
1) It is hot. (104°F)
2) 5 hours
3) 19.7 inches
4) 360 inches
5) 80 kilograms

Level 3

1) $3283\frac{1}{3}$ feet

2) 212°F
3) No (62.1 miles per hour)
4) 0°C
5) 3 meters

Einstein
1) 6 miles   Change 10,000 meters into inches.   Now divide by 12 to change inches into feet.   Now divide by 5280 to change to miles.

2) 38°C   Go in reverse through the changing machine. Subtract 32 and then divide by 1.8.

3) 89 kilometers per hour   Go in reverse through the changing machine. 55 divided by .621 equals 88.56682.

4) 37°C   Go in reverse through the changing machine. Subtract 32 and divide by 1.8.

5) $3600n$ The machine multiplies whatever you put through it by 3600.

Chapter 20

Level 1
1) Jackie: $n + 6$
2) Brother: $n + 9$
   Sister: $n + 1$
3) Dave: $n - 6$
4) Venus: $2n$
5) Cat: $3n$
   Dog: $n + 20$

Level 2
1) Mel: $n + 3$
   Emily: $2n + 6$
2) Bill: $3n + 42$
   Steve: $3n$
3) Minutes: $60n$
4) Inches: $36n$
5) Feet: $5280n$

Level 3
1) Yards: $n \div 3$
2) $25n$
3) Horse legs: $4n$
   Pig legs: 80
   Tripod: 3
   Total: $4n + 83$
4) Quarts: $4n$
   Pints: $8n$
   Cups: $16n$
5) Value of n nickels: $5n$

Einstein
1) Hours: $n \div 60$
2) Pigs: $75 - n$
3) Tom: $2n$
   Jordan: $n + 6$
   Laura: n
   Shadow: $n \div 3$

4) Decimeters: $10n$
   Centimeters: $100n$
   Millimeters: $1000n$
   Micron: $1,000,000n$
5) Cow legs: $4n$
   Duck legs: $2(50-n)$

   (The number of ducks is $50-n$
   so the number of legs is 2 times
   the number of ducks)

Chapter 21

Level 1
1) $n = 70$
2) $n = 50$
3) $n = 98$
4) $n = 4$
5) $n = 50$

Level 2
1) $n = 18$
2) $n = 10$
3) $n = 2$
4) $n = 25$
5) $n = 20$

Level 3
1) $n = 12$
2) $n = 5$
3) $n = 1$
4) $n = 3$
5) $n = 5$

Einstein
1) $n = 56$
2) $n = 4$
3) $n = 2$
4) $n = 30$
5) $n = -2\frac{1}{2}$

Chapter 22

Level 1
1) 10 years old
Language of algebra
Luke's age: $2n$
Brother's age: n

Equation: $3n = 15$
Answer: $n = 5$

2) 55 pounds
Language of algebra
Alex's weight: $n + 5$
Dog's weight: n

Equation: $2n + 5 = 105$
Answer: $n = 50$

3) $15
Language of algebra
Cost of mouse: $n + 5$
Cost of snake: n

Equation: $2n + 5 = 25$
Answer: $n = 10$

4) 4 feet
Language of algebra
Stanley's height: n
Giraffe's height: $n + 15$

Equation: $2n + 15 = 23$
Answer: $n = 4$

5) 5 pounds
Language of algebra
Einstein's weight: $n + 120$
Rat's weight: n

Equation: $2n + 120 = 130$
Answer: $n = 5$

Level 2

1) 35 pounds
Language of algebra
Dog: n
Anne: $n + 20$

Equation: $2n + 20 = 50$
Answer: $n = 15$

2) $12\frac{1}{2}$ pounds
Language of algebra
Steve's weight: n
Mom's weight: $n + 75$

Equation: $2n + 75 = 100$

Answer: $n = 12\frac{1}{2}$

3) 40 years old
Language of algebra
Ali's age: $2n$
Brother: n

Equation: $3n = 60$
Answer: $n = 20$

4) $3
Language of algebra
Adult ticket: $3n$
Child's ticket: n

Equation: $4n = 12$
Answer: $n = 3$

5) 27 inches
Language of algebra
Dan's height: $n + 35$
Baby's height: n

Equation: $2n + 35 = 89$
Answer: $n = 27$

Level 3
1) $30
Language of algebra
Mary's money: n
Lindsey's money: n
Sara's money: n
Rachel's money: 15

Equation: $3n + 15 = 105$
Answer: $n = 30$

2) $8
Language of algebra
Luke's money: n
Dan's money: n
Nick's money: n

Equation: $3n - 12 = 12$
Answer: $n = 8$

3) 2 pounds
Language of algebra
Weight of 1 math book: n

Equation: $7n + 8 = 22$
Answer: $n = 2$

4) $15
Language of algebra
Brother's gift: n
Dad's gift: $2n$
Mom's gift: $4n$

Equation: $7n = 105$
Answer: $n = 15$

5) 80 inches
Language of algebra
Mica's height: n
Kate's height: $2n$
Dave's height: $4n$

Equation: $7n = 140$
Answer: $n = 20$

Einstein
1) 1 year old
Language of algebra
Carly: $n + 9$
Stacie: $n + 5$
Ben: n

Equation: $3n + 14 = 17$
Answer: $n = 1$

2) Page 92
Language of algebra
Page sister is reading: n
Page before the one she is reading: $n - 1$
Page after the one she is reading: $n + 1$

Equation: $3n + 1 - 1 = 276$
Answer: $n = 92$

3) 32
Language of algebra
Mike's number: n

Equation: $3n = n + 64$
Answer: $n = 32$

4) 20 feet
Language of algebra
Width of rectangle: n
Length of rectangle: $3n$

Equation: $8n = 160$
Answer: $n = 20$

5) 20 quarters
Language of algebra
Number of nickels: n
Number of dimes: $2n$
Number of quarters: $5n$
Number of pennies: $2n$

Equation: $10n = 40$
Answer: $n = 4$

Chapter 23

Level 1
1) 5
2) 625
3) 36
4) 1
5) 10

Level 2
1) 49
2) 100
3) No
4) 1000
5) 50

Level 3
1) 1
2) 5 inches
3) 1/2
4) n
5) 1000

Einstein
1) 16
2) 2.5
3) 64
4) 3

5) 18 inches   The floor must be 1/2 yard by 1/2 yard because $\left(\dfrac{1}{2}\right)^2 = \dfrac{1}{4}$ sq. yards.

1/2 yard is equal to 18 inches.

Chapter 24

Level 1
1) 41 feet
2) 47.1 feet
3) 3.14 inches
4) 25,120 miles
5) 6280 miles

Level 2
1) $400
2) 9 square feet
3) 3140 seconds
4) 150 pounds
5) c) pi feet

Level 3
1) 1296 square inches
2) Yes
3) 90 tiles
4) 1682 feet
5) 202 tiles

Einstein
1) 20 feet   The diameter is found by dividing the circumference by π.
2) 1.14 miles   The distance around the lake is 6.28 miles. Ben would walk half of
                    that or 3.14 miles. 3.14 - 2 = 1.14 miles.
3) 1,570,000 miles 500,000 diameter of orbit times π = 1,570,000 miles.
4) Pi or 3.14
5) $3   There are 9 square feet in a square yard. 27 ÷ 9 = $3

Chapter 25

Level 1
1) Yes
2) No
3) The drawing with the small cats circle.
4) Yes
5) Yes

Level 2
1) Luke
2) No   We do not know if Alice cleaned her room or not. She may have lost her allowance for some other reason.
3) Angle A must be 90° or larger.
4) Yes   The statement says that if two conditions are met, the man will be cold. Both conditions are met.
5) No   He always wears his helmet when he is playing hockey. He may also wear it at other times------ like bike riding.

Level 3
1) No   A friend could have thrown a water balloon.
2) No   All people who dress in suits are popular, but many other people could be popular for other reasons.
3) No   Steve could be 6 years old and Claire 5. Mavis would then have to be 10 years old. Steve could also be 2 and Claire 1. Mavis would then have to be 2 years old.
4)
Step 1: Fill the 3 quart and pour it into the 5 quart.
Step 2: Fill the 3 quart again and pour 2 quarts into the 5 quart.
Step 3: Now there is 1 quart remaining in the 3 quart. Empty the 5 quart.
Step 4: Pour the 1 quart into the 5 quart.
Step 5: Fill the 3 quart and pour it into the 5.
There are now 4 quarts in the 5 quart container.
5) No   All teachers who picked blue are left-handed, but some left-handed teachers could have picked another color.

Einstein

1) Yes   If he drinks coffee he **will** get little sleep, which means he **will** fail the test. If he fails the test he **will not** get into his favorite college.

2)

Step 1: Fill the 7 quart and pour it into the 9 quart.

Step 2: Fill the 7 quart and pour 2 quarts into the 9 quart. The 9 quart is filled and 5 quarts are remaining in the 7 quart.

Step 3: Empty the 9 quart.

Step 4: Pour the remaining 5 quarts that are in the 7 quart into the 9 quart.

Step 5: Fill the 7 quart and pour 4 quarts into the 9 quart, which will fill it. 3 quarts are remaining in the 7 quart.

Step 6: Empty the 9 quart.

Step 7: Pour the 3 quarts that are remaining in the 7 quart into the 9 quart container.

Step 8: Fill the 7 quart and pour 6 quarts into the 9 quart. This will fill it and leave 1 quart remaining in the 7 quart container.

Step 9: Empty the 9 quart.

Step 10: Pour the 1 quart from the 7 quart into the 9 quart.

Step 11: Fill the 7 quart and pour it into the 9 quart.

There are now 8 quarts in the 9 quart container.

3) No   The reason they occur more often is because that is where people drive the most.

4) 8 miles   When you bike 12 miles, the tires go a total of 24 miles----12 miles each tire. If you want each of the 3 tires to go an equal amount, then they will each go 8 miles.

5) 27 rungs

Chapter 26

Level 1
1) 6
2) b) Hundredths
3) Put the money through the hundredths machine. After it is cut into 100 equal pieces, they would each take 22 of the pieces.
4) .7 of the pie
5) .8 of the pie

Level 2
1) .4
2) If you divide a dollar into 100 parts, each part is worth a penny. The answer is 47¢
3) 10 pieces
4) 100 pieces
5) Dime

Level 3
1) $\dfrac{4}{10} + \dfrac{2}{100}$
2) .1
3) $10
4) $\dfrac{7}{10} + \dfrac{9}{100} + \dfrac{8}{1000}$
5) .72 of the pie

Einstein
1) .100001
2) 100 pounds.   50 tons = 100,000 pounds. 100,000 pounds divided by 1000 equals 100 pounds.
3) 10,000 pieces
4) $\dfrac{8}{10} + \dfrac{4}{100} + \dfrac{9}{1000} + \dfrac{2}{10,000}$
5) .6125

Chapter 27

Level 1
1) 1/2   .5
2) 1/4   .25
3) 3/4   75%
4) 90%   .9
5) 10%   1/10

Level 2
1) 20%   .2
2) 100%
3) .05   5/100 or 1/20
4) 30%   3/10
5) 1/100

Level 3
1) 2/1 or 4/2 or 6/3 etc.
2) 60%   .6
3) 2/100 or 1/50
4) 99/100   .99
5) 5

Einstein
1) 1/200   .005
2) 1.01
3) 1/3   .33
4) $1\frac{1}{2}$ 1.5
5) Yes   50% is 100 times larger than .5%